Copyright © 2021

No part of this publication may be reproduced, stored in a retrieval system, or transmitted in any form or by any means, electronic, mechanical, photocopying, recording, scanning, or otherwise. Limit of Liability/Disclaimer of Warranty: The Publisher and the author make no representations or warranties with respect to the accuracy or completeness of the contents of this work and specifically disclaim all warranties, including without limitation warranties of fitness for a particular purpose. No warranty may be created or extended by sales or promotional materials. The advice and strategies contained herein may not be suitable for every situation. This work is sold with the understanding that the Publisher is not engaged in rendering medical, legal, or other professional advice or services. If professional assistance is required, the services of a competent professional person should be sought. Neither the Publisher nor the author shall be liable for damages arising herefrom. The fact that an individual, organization, or website is referred to in this work as a citation and/or potential source of further information does not mean that the author or the Publisher endorses the information the individual, organization, or website may provide or recommendations they/it may make. Further, readers should be aware that websites listed in this work may have changed or disappeared between when this work was written and when it is read.

contents

Introduction

Part One: Training Fundamentals and Puppy Prep

CHAPTER 1 Training Fundamentals

CHAPTER 2 Puppy Supplies Checklist

CHAPTER 3 Puppy-Proof Your Home

Part Two: The Training Steps

STEP 1 Bringing Your Puppy Home

STEP 2 Crate Training

STEP 3 Potty Training

STEP 4 Preventing Food Aggression

STEP 5 Socializing Your Puppy

STEP 6 The Six Key Commands

STEP 7 Leash Walking and Coming When Called

Preparing for the Future

Resources

Introduction

To understand how we came to write this book, it's helpful to know a little about who we are. The Zoom Room is an indoor dog training gym with locations around the United States and more on the way. We practice only positive reinforcement training methods, which are central to the philosophy of this book. We're not a day care or drop-off facility. We celebrate puppy and dog owners who want to learn, play, and sweat alongside their pups, deepening the bonds of communication.

The inspiration for this book really comes from the Zoom Room's motto:

We don't train dogs. We train the people who love them.

Our expertise isn't simply dog training; rather, it's our ability to be great communicators—to teach every dog owner to better understand their dog's perspective, behavior, and body language; to know why they're doing what they're doing, not merely how to change their behavior or train a command.

And that's also our goal with this book: to impart to you not only the step-by-step knowledge of how to get your puppy to do this or that (or *not* do, as the case may be), but to shed light on *why* you're going to follow these steps and *why* they work and what this all means to your new puppy.

We love puppies. We offer puppy preschool, puppy obedience classes, puppy agility classes, puppy playgroups, and even puppy Pup-lates® (core conditioning for canines) throughout the week, along with classes for adult dogs. But we begin every weekend morning with puppy preschool because there is no better way to enjoy your weekend than with a roomful of puppies and their owners.

The clients get to socialize and bond with each other, too, and most of them have the same questions and concerns, and find true camaraderie in hearing about each other's foibles, mishaps, and triumphs. The questions and information that we've heard from over 100,000 clients in our 10-plus-year history were a tremendous source of inspiration for this book. We've learned exactly what's on the mind of new puppy owners who are looking to train their puppy.

Something you might notice is that we use the words *owner* and *client*, and not *pet parent*. We also refer to their companions as puppies and dogs, not as *fur babies*. But we don't say *owner* because we think of dogs as chattel. Far from it. We spend every day experiencing the unconditional love that dogs bring into our lives. The reason is that it is far too easy to anthropomorphize puppies and call them *fur babies* or *four-legged children* and in the process forget the wonderful, remarkable fact that you're now sharing your home with a wholly other species.

We celebrate the dogginess of dogs and the puppiness of puppies. They aren't kids. They do have enormous personalities, profound emotions, and big brains. They have puppy hearts and minds. And we need to remember this, understand this, and love them for working with us to bridge the enormous language and culture barrier that separates humans and canines.

What is a puppy? This might seem a ridiculous question, but we have had so many people call us to say they want to bring their puppy in for training and when we ask the puppy's age, we hear, "Oh, my puppy is two years old."

We define a puppy as a juvenile dog between the ages of birth and one year, the point at which the majority of dogs have reached sexual maturity and thus adolescence. This book will focus primarily on puppies between two and six months old.

Age matters for puppies because they're operating within fairly brief developmental windows. It's only during the first few months that a puppy's brain is plastic, meaning that its connections are still being formed. The more plastic the brain, the greater the opportunity for a puppy to learn.

The majority of people get their new puppy around eight weeks of age. It's for this audience that this book is intended. If you've adopted a six-month-old puppy from a shelter or rescue who requires basic training, that puppy has likely suffered at least some neglect and will probably arrive with some behavioral and trust issues and attachment disorders. This book can help you deepen your understanding and can provide some helpful tips, but this book (or any book) isn't going to suffice. You'll benefit from the help of a professional trainer. Potty training a six-month-old is very different from doing so with an eight-week-old.

Beyond the owners of puppies of a certain age, who is this book for?

It's for first-time puppy owners and those getting a new puppy who wouldn't mind a little refresher. It's for those who are committed to positive training and willing to exercise all the necessary patience and restraint to shelter their puppy from the inevitable frustrations you might feel. And it's for those who are willing and able to set aside the time and give the attention needed to properly raise and train a puppy. Throughout the book you'll see reminders of the importance of attentiveness and supervision.

If your schedule is such that your new puppy is going to be home alone for more than a few hours during the day on a regular basis, we'd ask you to reconsider bringing a puppy into your home, unless you have a plan in place that makes liberal use of dog walkers, friends, or neighbors to fill in the gaps when you're gone.

We know that life can be full and busy. This book offers a training plan that will help you manage a life that includes this incredible new family member. And throughout, we'll provide assistance on when and how to leave your puppy with thoughtful confinement, and also about how to take your puppy with you out into the world.

We know that every puppy owner wants to have a well-adjusted, emotionally stable dog who is friendly, happy, and able to serve as a super fun companion on many of your outings. And for that reason, we're going to emphasize the role of early socialization—and plenty of it—throughout these pages.

This book will provide you with everything you need to know to get your house ready for your puppy, to crate and potty train them, to socialize them, and to teach them basic obedience, all in seven simple steps. The steps themselves are easy, and your puppy *will* learn. But do prepare yourself for challenges—challenges to your ability to remain patient, consistent, and positive in the presence of juvenile rambunctiousness and wanton destruction. But we're going to be right there with you, every step of the way.

part one

Training Fundamentals and Puppy Prep

Well, what can we say but *congratulations*! You're about to bring a new puppy home, and your life will never be the same. This is certainly cause for celebration, but also a time to reflect on the immensity of the journey ahead. You're about to share your home with a totally different species.

Your new best friend doesn't speak your language, at least not yet. Your puppy doesn't know their own name. Or where they're supposed to go to the bathroom. Or what the difference is between the chew toys you've lovingly picked out and your very best pair of shoes.

Puppies might not know much, but they have a lot of questions, unbridled curiosity, tons of energy, and a whole universe to explore. Good thing they have you.

Within the pages of this book, you'll learn how to set your relationship up for success as you build your new life together.

First things first. Let's get to know more about this newest family member, and let's get your home all set up for your puppy's imminent arrival.

CHAPTER 1

training fundamentals

Training is no different than teaching. And in order to teach successfully, excellent communication is needed. Communication is a two-way street; your puppy's brain is going to be working overtime to understand this bizarre language you speak with lots of words and a total absence of butt sniffing. But you'll need to put in the effort, too, to understand their native language and drives, and to create the perfect atmosphere for learning. Our **Seven Tenets of Puppy Training** are the cardinal concepts that lay the groundwork. Please note that these concepts all apply equally to adult dogs as well.

Seven Tenets of Puppy Training

1. POSITIVITY

Positive reinforcement simply means that when your dog exhibits the behavior you want, you reward them. Period. (No one said this was rocket science.) Countless scientific studies have established that positive rewards are the single most effective method for dog training. As a bonus, it's easy and fun and every member of your household can take part. In Socializing Your Puppy, we'll explain the methods of training with positive rewards.

   Positivity also means a generosity of spirit and kindness. You're going to keep things light and upbeat, always. If you try to dominate or act aggressively toward your puppy, they'll develop mistrust, a lack of affection, and perhaps even aggression. See yourself the way you want them to see you: as their *benevolent leader*. Yes, you make the rules. But you do so with a gentle hand that offers treats and petting.

2. CONSISTENCY

Consistency means repetition. That's how all creatures learn: train, repeat, train, repeat. And your puppy will learn fast. You may have heard or experienced that dogs are creatures of habit. And you're now in the business of shaping and developing good habits that work for you. An important part of consistency is teaching your puppy *your* schedule, rather than you learning theirs.

3. PATIENCE

Let's be realistic: You're not going to be patient with your puppy simply because patience is a virtue. It has utility, too. Consider training your puppy with an *absence* of patience: Do this, and the training just won't take. Your frustration will cause them to become frustrated, and can also lead to a lack of learning, bad behaviors, and aggression.

To truly embody patience takes constantly reminding yourself that what you and your puppy are doing is nothing short of astonishing. You're teaching a dog to understand another language. Take a minute to marvel at this.

Now, having marveled, temper your expectations. In dog training, it's very often two steps forward and one step back. Remember: it's usually us who are making things tough. We might use two different commands instead of one, or alter our tone of voice, or make other subtle changes in how we train, which can throw a puppy for a loop. Don't demand too much from them. Remain patient. You will master all of this, and so will they. It just takes time. Expect the setbacks, remind yourself of the amazingness of what you're accomplishing, and keep going.

4. TIMING

Here's an area where your puppy is extremely different than you. A dog's brain is unique in that they have a tiny window (about 1.5 seconds) in which to associate an action with its consequence. If you left the toilet seat up last night, and this morning someone mentions to you that they didn't appreciate it, you understand. You can learn. But a puppy can't. Not unless it was less than 1.5 seconds ago. If your puppy peed on the floor 10 minutes ago and you show it to them and say, "Look what you did," they have no idea what you're talking about. Same goes for good behaviors. If your puppy sits, and you wait a few seconds before rewarding them and letting them know they did the right thing, the training has been lost on them. In The Six Key Commands, we'll give you all the tools you need to work within this tight timing.

Timing also means knowing when to train and when not to train. You need to be able to read the room. You'll develop the ability to assess your puppy's current level of activity and focus. Knowing whether they're hungry is also important in choosing the right time to train. You will be able to evaluate the potential distractions in an environment. Sometimes you want to have a moderately distracting environment; other times, you won't.

5. SOCIALIZATION

There's a reason why the chapter on socializing in this book comes before the one on basic training. Socializing your puppy isn't merely important, it's actually *more* important than training. Why? Consider this: Ask anyone what they'd like in a dog, and the answer you *won't* hear is a dog who can sit, stay, and lie down. Instead, people will say they want a happy dog. A calm dog. A stable dog who they can take out in public without being worried that they will bark, nip, bolt, or create a nuisance.

How do you get a happy, stable dog? It's not through training commands. It's via socialization, and plenty of it. You actually have a very short window—a mere eight weeks between the ages of eight weeks old and 16 weeks old—to make the biggest difference in the life of your future adult dog. In Socializing Your Puppy, we'll give you lots more information about how to make the most of these eight weeks to set the stage for a very happy life together.

6. UNDERSTANDING

Your puppy isn't a baby human. They're a different species with their own drives, body language, and repertoire of doggy speech and idiosyncrasies. In short: Get to know your puppy. Reading this book is an excellent first step, and we've included a Puppy Perspective in each of the training steps to help you understand these motivations.

The better you can understand not simply what puppies do but *why* they do what they do, the better equipped you'll be to become the benevolent leader of a gloriously well-adjusted pup.

7. SAFETY

While it's true your puppy is no delicate flower—and many puppy owners are far too sensitive and precious about the little bonks and mishaps that are quite natural and that your puppy can easily withstand—they do need looking after.

Regular vet visits are important. If your puppy is sick or injured, taking them to the vet is of paramount importance. But most of what you can do for your puppy's well-being is to anticipate the kinds of trouble they can get into due to their limitless curiosity and their drive to chew anything and jump on everything, and then take the necessary precautions.

Puppy-Proof Your Home will pave the way for your puppy's safety by helping you prep your home for their arrival.

CHAPTER 2

puppy supplies checklist

Time to go shopping. You'll want to take care of all purchases ahead of time so that on the day your puppy comes home everything will already be in place.

We think it's important to be mindful of the expenses of pet ownership, so we've focused on the essentials and included some cost-saving examples of stuff that you *don't* actually want to purchase, as it will be far too likely to be quickly destroyed at this age. And everything on our list will be easy to find in your favorite local or online retailer; some you may even be able to pick up used.

So, with that said, here's a handy list of all the necessities (and some optional items) for your puppy.

Crate Training Supplies

This is the necessary equipment to crate train and thoughtfully confine your puppy to keep them safe.

CRATE

Purchase a crate that will accommodate your puppy when they are full grown, rather than buying a small one now and having to buy larger ones in the future. Make sure you get one that comes with dividers that allow you to limit the interior dimensions. As your puppy grows, you'll move the dividers accordingly. Your puppy should fit snugly inside, with sufficient room for them to lie down but no larger, as that would interfere with potty training.

Avoid fabric crates, as a puppy will chew through them. Metal crates come with a plastic tray at the base, or you can purchase a plastic crate.

CRATE MAT

Avoid the temptation to purchase an adorable dog bed or an expensive crate mat or pad for your puppy at first, as they'll get trashed through chewing and soiling. A crate mat is a necessity, but use something cheap and easy to wash. Popular options are old towels or blankets, or even old T-shirts. You want them to have soft padding inside the crate, but it's wise to wait for your puppy to be trained before buying their first dog bed.

SAFETY HARNESS AND STRAPS

If your crate is too large to fit in your car when transporting your puppy, you will need a safety harness to safely restrain them. If your crate does fit, you should anchor it with straps.

GATES

Puppies need containment. Not just for their safety and your peace of mind, but also because puppies fare better in smaller areas. Puppy gates are really no different than baby gates, and they can be used interchangeably. You'll either need enough gates for the areas of your home that might need closing off, or you'll want a movable gate that you can pick up and reinstall when you switch rooms or floors. Initially, your puppy should be limited to only a single room at a time, such as the kitchen.

PEN

Pens are highly recommended for everyone, but an absolute must if your schedule will necessitate leaving your puppy home alone for more than a few hours at a time. If you're gone that long, you can't leave them in their crate the whole time because they'll need access to water and a potty area.

Purchase a pen that is high enough to contain your puppy once they are full grown. Pens are typically made of metal and easily fold flat for transport. The mobility of a pen is especially handy when you go over to a friend or family member's home and want to bring your puppy with you. Your friend likely won't have a pen, and by bringing one you'll be able to help out with dinner in the kitchen while your puppy is safe in their penned-in area. The pen will also allow your friends to step inside and play with the puppy and their toys.

BITTER APPLE

An unpleasant-tasting spray such as bitter apple can be used as an effective deterrent when sprayed on a potential hazard such as an electrical cord. Such sprays may only ever be used on objects as a passive deterrent. Never use any aversive spray on your dog or as a component of an active training session.

Leash Walking Supplies

Here's everything you need to safely take your puppy out on their first walk and train them to love their leash.

COLLAR

Find any flat-buckle collar you like. The design is up to you. All that matters is that it has a breakaway design, as the majority of flat-buckle collars do. This means that if the collar gets snagged on something, the buckle will break open to prevent your puppy getting injured.

FRONT-CLIP HARNESS

We'll discuss this item more in Leash Walking and Coming When Called. For now, go ahead and buy a front-clip harness that fits your puppy. Front clip means you attach the leash clasp to the front of the harness along the strap that goes across your puppy's chest. Do not buy a harness where you attach the leash to a strap on top of your puppy's back, as this can trigger a reflex causing them to pull harder when you walk. Note that while they are adjustable in size, harnesses can only be adjusted up to a limit. Unless you have a very small breed, it's more likely than not that you will end up needing to purchase another, larger-size harness as your puppy grows. With the largest of breeds, you might end up purchasing three.

I.D. TAG

Have a personalized collar tag made before you pick your puppy up. Include your puppy's name and your phone number.

LEASH

You'll need a six-foot leash. It can be leather, nylon, hemp—the material doesn't matter. What does matter is that you *do not* get a retractable leash. Retractable leashes pose numerous risks to you and your puppy's safety. For more on retractable leashes, see The Dangers of Retractable Leashes.

HOUSE LINE

This is an optional but recommended training item. The benefit of a house line (also known as a puppy line) is that it gets your puppy accustomed to the feeling of wearing a leash, which, when you stop and think about it, is a pretty bizarre way to walk around if you've never done it before. A house line is much like a leash, but it has no handle. Your puppy wears it around the house. It's that simple.

If you decide to go this route, purchase an eight-foot house line. Resist the temptation to just use their leash; we never recommend this as the leash's handle very easily gets caught on furniture, door corners, and other items, which can injure your puppy. Don't improvise any old string or rope, the weight of which might alter your puppy's natural gait. Purchase a house line intended for this purpose.

The Dangers of Retractable Leashes

While retractable leashes have become very popular, they pose numerous safety hazards for you and your puppy.

- They give you a false sense of control.
- When extended and the leash drags on the ground, this can frighten a puppy.
- Retractable leashes allow the dog to control the walk instead of you.
- They get caught in bushes, hydrants, and other obstacles.
- Your legs can get tangled up in the cord, and when the dog bolts, you can be knocked off your feet and injured.
- They extend such a long distance that a dog on such a "leash" can actually run right into the street or greet an unknown dog. Your reflexes are only so fast, and if your dog on an extended leash does run into danger, such as a strange dog, there won't be enough time for you to reel them in.
- The leash itself isn't truly a leash but rather a thin cord that can snap under the pressure of a larger dog lunging or running. That thin cord has caused significant human injuries. When people need to quickly reel in the dog, they tend to grab the cord, which can cause the hand to be burned so severely as to require surgery or even amputation.
- Furthermore, many states have laws prohibiting the use of retractable leashes; if a law requires that a dog be on a six-foot leash or shorter, a retractable leash is considered illegal. Always stick to a nonretractable leash for all puppies and all adult dogs.

Potty Training Supplies

Accidents will happen. Here's what you need to contain the mess.

POTTY PADS

Whether you call them puppy pads or wee wee pads, they're essentially high-quality flattened diapers that you place on the floor during potty training. They are extremely absorbent and have a plastic underside to prevent leakage, protecting your floor. Most come with a built-in pheromone attractant that entices your puppy to pee on them. Others come with an attractant spray sold separately. Either option is fine, but obviously the one with the built-in attractant is more convenient.

If you're wondering if you could use old newspapers instead, we regret to inform you that this is the twenty-first century. In all seriousness, don't use them, even if you have them, for they lack the absorbency and leakproof plastic casing of potty pads, and your puppy's mess will seep into your floor.

CLEANING SUPPLIES

Dogs love to pee where there's pee. They detect this using their phenomenally keen sense of smell. If you think normal household soap and a sponge will work, you're thinking only of the visual mess; those pheromones will linger behind as if you had never cleaned.

That's why you need cleaning products specially designed for pet mess. The best ones all use enzymes to encapsulate and gobble up the odors that we might miss but your puppy will certainly notice.

Arm yourself with an enzyme-based pet odor spray and an enzyme-based stain remover. You're also going to need way more paper towels than you might anticipate. Purchase those in bulk.

POOP BAGS

Even if you have a yard and plan to use a pooper scooper, get a supply of bags for when you're out and about with your puppy. We always recommend biodegradable pet waste bags. Some people like to purchase a handy poop bag dispenser that can be clipped to a leash handle.

POOPER SCOOPER

An optional item for those with yards.

Feeding and Grooming Supplies

Keep your pup growing strong and healthy with proper nutrition and grooming care.

FOOD

Purchase the best quality food that you can afford. Dog foods vary widely. The most inexpensive foods tend to have far fewer calories per cup of food and therefore require larger servings—and produce much larger poops.

There are several "dog food calculators" online that do a good job of comparing apples to apples; the classic mistake is to price shop by comparing costs for a bag of food. You're better off comparing cost per serving or cost per calorie. Do this and you may be surprised to find that some of the more inexpensive foods are actually not less expensive in the long run.

Different breeds of puppies have varying dietary needs with regard to the amount of specific nutrients required. Large-breed puppies require food that is explicitly labeled "Large Breed Puppy Formula" due to their rapid rate of growth. For all other puppies—small or medium breeds—you may opt either for food labeled "Puppy Formula" or "All Life Stages Formula." Food labeled "All Life Stages Formula" has been verified to contain all the nutrition an adult dog needs, plus all the special nutrients a small- or medium-breed puppy requires.

There is an enormous variety of dog and puppy food on the market now, including kibble, wet or canned, raw that is dehydrated (you add water), raw that is fresh or frozen, and raw that is freeze dried or air dried. All of these are perfectly fine for your puppy, so let your budget and cost per serving aid you in the decision. On the other hand, table scraps are not nutritionally appropriate for your puppy and are the gateway to terrible habits such as begging during meals and counter-surfing (when your dog jumps up on the counter and grabs any food they can).

FOOD AND WATER DISHES

Just about any dishes are fine—metal, ceramic, or enamel. Only plastic should be avoided, as over time it starts to splinter and can embed tiny bits of plastic in your dog's tongue and mouth. Both bowls should be cleaned daily to avoid contamination from bacteria. If it's easier for you, purchase dishwasher-safe bowls.

Some puppies and dogs are messy eaters or drinkers. There's not much you can do about this, but if you're feeling frustrated, you can purchase a place mat or feeding mat to put underneath their dishes. If your puppy makes a mess with their water, be sure your chosen mat has raised edges to keep the water contained.

There is one special option that we very often recommend to our clients: slow bowls. (For food only, not water.) A slow bowl can come in many designs, but it always turns mealtime into a bit of a puzzle. The kibble falls into grooves, nooks, or crannies so your puppy has to really work to get at their meal. As the name implies, slow bowls slow down the rate of eating, which aids in your puppy's digestion.

Many people misunderstand how wonderful slow bowls are. They might think: Hey, that's mean. Why are you making your little puppy work so hard for their supper? But slow bowls actually appeal to the canine mind.

By nature, dogs are scavengers. They love looking for food. Having to dig around and hunt for the pieces of kibble engages this hereditary impulse to scavenge and stimulates genuine pleasure. It is fun for them, not mean. You're giving your dog dinner and entertainment that's good for their brain. See more on this with regard to Puzzle Toys.

GROOMING SUPPLIES

You'll want a brush, a nail trimmer (Dremel or clipper), styptic powder for dogs (in case of accidental cuts when trimming nails), ear cleaning solution or wipes, and pet shampoo. Accept no substitute for a dedicated pet shampoo that is pH balanced specifically for dogs. Human shampoo or dishwashing liquid will harm your puppy's skin and coat.

You'll also want dental health products. There is now a wide variety of good options including toothbrush, toothpaste, special dental chews, tablets, and other items.

Lastly, for breeds prone to leaky tear ducts, you should get eye wipes. Pekingese, Maltese, Poodles, Cocker Spaniels, and Pugs are just some of the breeds for which this tends to be an issue.

Treats and Toys

Last but not least, you'll want to stock up on treats and chew toys to aid with training.

TREATS FOR TRAINING

Not all omnivores are alike. Dogs, for example, are carnivore/omnivores, at the super meaty end of the spectrum. In positive reinforcement training, you're going to need plenty of enticing treats. They should be soft, tiny, and primarily made out of pure meat with very little filler, if any. High protein, low calorie. Larger training treats are only okay if you can very easily tear them into tiny pieces with your hands.

TREAT POUCH

Trainable moments can happen anytime, anywhere. Having a treat pouch (also called a bait bag) on your hip and filled with training treats means you're always prepared to seize that moment. We recommend the ones with a hinged or magnetic closure; we dislike the drawstring option as it causes too much fumbling. A resealable plastic baggie also works, but a treat pouch gives you maximum speed and convenience.

TREATS FOR CHEWING

Avoid rawhide. Rawhide poses numerous health and safety risks to puppies and dogs and should always be avoided. Thankfully, there are some wonderful safe alternatives to rawhide on the market. You can also use a wide range of other natural chews such as trachea, bully sticks, pig ears, tendons, dried sweet potato wedges, and hard cheese chews. While naturally shed antlers are also a good option, for puppies stick to split antlers, not whole ones. For puppies, the rule for chews is that they should all be fully digestible; rawhide is not.

Around four months of age, when your puppy starts losing their puppy teeth, they'll need to stick to softer chews such as tendons and sweet potatoes. No split antler, bully sticks, or hard cheese chews.

Don't leave your puppy unsupervised with these chews until you know their habits well. Watch them and make sure they're chewing and playing safely with them, predictably so, before you leave them alone with a given type of chew.

CHEW TOYS AND TUGS

There are tons of fun toys and tugs out there, made from all kinds of materials. Just avoid anything that shreds, splinters, or has little plastic pieces that can break off.

There's nothing wrong with stuffed toys as long as you understand that your puppy might destroy them. If that notion has you seeing visions of dollar bills tumbling into a fire pit, avoid toys with stuffing or stick to ones designed for strong chewers. If it will amuse you to watch them have a blast ripping the innards out of a cute little stuffed animal, go for it.

Chewing is extra important for puppies because they are teething. Teething happens when the adult teeth are pushing through the gums, and it's the gum irritation that makes them want to chew, chew, chew. This teething period typically happens between three and five months of age. During this time, stick to toys labeled "good for teething."

Remember, don't leave your puppy alone with chew toys until you've seen firsthand that they play safely with them.

PUZZLE TOYS

At the Zoom Room, puzzle toys are one of our absolute favorite things to provide to puppy and dog owners. We are huge fans of mental stimulation, and a good puzzle toy does wonders for a curious puppy or adult dog. Dogs can be creative, imaginative problem solvers, and a puzzle toy allows them to exercise their brains in a fun fashion, with the reward built right in.

Puzzle toys come in many different designs, but all possess some aspect of secreting treats inside, and your puppy must identify the trick to getting at them.

Some puzzle toys are incredibly simple: nothing more than a hollow center that you can stuff with treats or a combination of treats, peanut butter, and dog food. Others are bona fide games in which you can adjust the difficulty level.

One of our favorite tips for our clients is to use puzzle toys to give your dog their entire meal. Used in this fashion, puzzle toys have all the same benefits as a slow bowl. Many puzzles involve rolling the toy around, which provides some exercise for your puppy as well. And since puppies require a lot of exercise, it's beneficial to get that extra romp.

As with the other toys and chews mentioned, don't leave your puppy unsupervised with a puzzle toy until you've witnessed firsthand that they are using it safely.

Adding Variety to Your Puppy's Diet

A common misperception among dog owners is that it's bad for your dog to switch their food, and that you should stick with one food forever. In reality, variety is just as important to your puppy's diet as it is for your own. It's more than the spice of life. Adult dogs can develop allergies if they are overexposed to one single protein source such as chicken. There's no good reason to force a monoculture diet on your puppy.

Their first experience with variety should be on their first day in your home. Get some of the food they'd been eating before you got them and mix it with the new food you've selected for them, until they've fully made the transition over a few days or a week.

Although giant bags of dog food tend to be less expensive than smaller ones, for puppies we recommend buying small- or medium-size bags. Assuming this food is working well for your puppy, as soon as they finish the bag switch to a different variety of food in the same line of dog food. If they just finished a bag where salmon is the main protein, their next bag should be chicken, pork, beef, or whitefish, whatever options that brand offers.

The myth about switching dog foods causing tummy upsets is only true when you radically shift the quality or nature of ingredients or if your puppy is genetically predisposed to having a sensitive stomach. For example, a low-end dog food might have a preponderance of carbs and fillers. Switching to a food that has way more protein—a totally different formula—could indeed cause some stomach trouble, so in such a case you should transition from one food to the next over a four- to seven-day period.

CHAPTER 3

puppy-proof your home

When it comes to puppies, accidents *will* happen. It's 100 percent guaranteed your puppy will pee in your house, knock things over, jump on furniture, and chew things. This chapter will help you prepare your home for those inevitable accidents. But also remember to prepare yourself mentally, and that goes equally for everyone who lives in your household. You must remain patient, tolerant, understanding, and benevolent. Not simply because those are wonderful values, but because if you slip into anger and frustration, your puppy is unlikely to learn any useful lessons and likely to learn to mistrust you or people in general. Now is when they are the most impressionable. So, let's prepare your home and mind.

Move Breakables and Valuables

It may take a little getting used to, but moving breakables to higher shelves and putting away objects of value will help you keep your cool when your puppy is overly rambunctious.

BREAKABLES

In The Six Key Commands, we'll discuss training your puppy not to jump up. But even if they're not jumping, their tail is bound to be wagging. Puppies are bundles of energy: think of the Tasmanian Devil. Before you bring them home, envision a mini tornado running and bonking and jostling into each piece of furniture. Take everything breakable and move it to higher ground. Securing items with earthquake putty is effective, too. If you wear eyeglasses, get in the habit of always placing them on a high counter whenever you set them down. Ditto for wineglasses or any other breakables you might normally set down on a low coffee table.

VALUABLES

The classic example of a puppy ruining your valuables is chewing your shoes. Puppies have an innate drive to chew things. Get everyone in the household used to the new rule of keeping shoes in a closet (and closing the closet door) or in a lidded bin. But cast the net well beyond shoes—beloved stuffed animals (that to the puppy look just like their new stuffed toys), decorative plates, jewelry, and other items. Your house is about to get a whole lot tidier. Keep everything stowed away.

RUGS AND CARPETS

Until your puppy is housebroken, anticipate that they're going to pee on the floor. If you have rugs you can easily roll up and store until they're trained, do so. If you have wall-to-wall carpeting in certain rooms, consider keeping them out of those rooms until they're trained. If carpet is everywhere, a great enzyme-based odor spray and a stain remover are your new best friends.

Remove Hazards

From chokeables to poisons, you'll want to be sure your puppy's indoor and outdoor living spaces are hazard-free zones.

CHOKING HAZARDS

While this section is entitled "Choking Hazards," the truth is that if your puppy gobbles a LEGO or a marble or a quarter or an earring, it is very unlikely that they will choke. Far more likely is that they will swallow it and eventually pass it. You know what we're talking about. Your fishing expedition is going to be gross, but your puppy will probably be just fine.

Choking can happen, but it can happen even when they're eating dinner, training treats, or a chew. This is precisely why we don't leave puppies alone when they are eating or playing with toys or chews until we know how they will interact with those items. We all know that even as grown-ups, occasionally we are eating and something goes down the wrong pipe and we choke.

A choking puppy will cough and retch and will usually be able to expel the object successfully on their own. However, if they are truly choking and their airway is blocked, a trip to the vet won't happen fast enough. See Choking First Aid so you know what to do.

Choking First Aid

Normally, a puppy's natural gag reflex will help them bring up anything that may have gotten stuck. Coughing and gagging may look like choking but won't prevent your puppy from engaging in normal activities. If they are truly choking, they will likely act extremely anxious with their stomach muscles visibly tightening as they try desperately to inhale. They will have halted all other activities in this state of panic. Most likely the attempt to inhale will be silent or you may hear a high whistling sound, and you might also notice pallor in the lips and gums. If your puppy is choking, follow the first aid protocol below.

1. Place one hand on their upper jaw, the other on their lower jaw, and pry their mouth open, squeezing the lips between your fingers and the puppy's teeth.

2. Look inside their mouth to see if there is an obviously obstructing object protruding. If so, remove this with your hand. If you *cannot* clearly view the obstruction, do not dig or sweep around inside their mouth or throat. If freeing the object by hand isn't working, abandon the effort, as time is of the essence.

3. If you're unable to remove the object and your puppy is breathing—even if labored—rush to the nearest veterinarian.

4. If your puppy cannot breathe, and if they're small enough, pick them up by their rear feet and shake two or three times in a downward motion.

5. If this does not work, or if your puppy is larger, you will need to perform the canine equivalent of the Heimlich maneuver. If you can lift them, raise them so their back is flat against your chest and sharply squeeze their chest backward toward your own chest until the object pops out.

6. For larger puppies, lean over or kneel down and hug them from above, wrapping your arms around their lower chest area. Now squeeze and thrust upward just below the rib cage in a slightly forward motion until the object is expelled.

ELECTRICAL HAZARDS

Know that your puppy will view all electrical cords as chew toys. This is one of the most common serious injuries that befall puppies. Take preventive measures. Examine all cords in your home and if you find any damaged or frayed cords, replace them. All cords should be completely inaccessible to your puppy. Stow them inside furniture cabinets or behind furniture or run them along walls and cover them with electrical tape. Instead of tape, you can also purchase special cord-hiding strips from any office supply store. You can also use a folding pen as a barrier to surround an area with lots of cords, such as a TV entertainment system or computer desk. As an added measure, you can keep any appliances you're not using unplugged. If a puppy chews an unplugged cord, the cord will be damaged, but not your puppy.

Electrical cords may also be treated with bitter apple (see the Puppy Supplies Checklist). Bitter food–based sprays are safe and effective at preventing chewing and can be sprayed on almost any surface you are worried about your puppy damaging, such as electrical cords, chair legs, and table legs. The taste is so repulsive that the vast majority of puppies will avoid any object on which it's been sprayed.

POISONS

Cleaning Supplies and Medications

Keep your puppy away from all household toxins. The most common poisons are household cleaning supplies, which must always be secured in a cabinet. Medication is the second most common. Assume that every single pill, capsule, patch, or liquid that anyone in your household takes, whether prescription or over-the-counter, is dangerous to a puppy if ingested. Keep all of them in drawers or cabinets where your puppy can't get to them.

Household Plants

Less obvious than cleaning supplies and medicine are household plants. There's an exhaustive list of plants toxic to dogs on the ASPCA's website (see Resources, for more information). The most common poisonous plants are azalea, daffodil, autumn crocus, dieffenbachia, tulip, sago palm, oleander, amaryllis, aloe, calla lily, bird of paradise, jade plant, Kaffir lily, and desert rose. If you have these plants in your yard, you should get rid of them. If they're inside, move them to higher ground where your dog can't possibly reach them, or to be safe, find a new home for them.

Human Food

What about human food? Most people know chocolate is bad for dogs, but it's actually rarely life threatening. Still, you do want to keep your puppy away from all chocolate—the darker the chocolate, the more toxic it is for them. Grapes, raisins, onions, garlic, and macadamia nuts all are toxic for your puppy. In recent years, the most common human food that causes illness in dogs is sugarless candy and gum containing xylitol. Your puppy can experience serious damage if they ingest xylitol, so don't leave a purse containing sugarless gum in your home or car where they could root around and get into trouble. See Resources for more information.

Alcohol and Drugs

One of the *most* toxic substances for dogs is alcohol. Dogs are incredibly sensitive to alcohol, and it's never okay to give them even a tiny sip. Hops are also very toxic to dogs, so beer is extremely poisonous. Recently, many states have changed their laws regarding marijuana use for humans. Regardless of your state's laws, it's important to know that THC, one of the active ingredients in marijuana, is highly toxic to dogs. Conversely, CBD, another active ingredient in marijuana that has no psychotropic effect, is regularly used to treat a variety of medical and behavioral issues in dogs. Dogs can only safely consume CBD products specifically designed for use in pets and only after consulting with your vet. They should never be given any other type of marijuana.

OUTDOORS

Depending on where you live, you may need to do some additional puppy-proofing in the exterior areas of your home such as your yard, driveway, or garage. Let's go over the dangers you should keep in mind when exposing your puppy to the outdoors.

Poisons

Antifreeze is the most common deadly poison that can seriously harm or even kill a puppy, because it unfortunately tastes delicious to them. Make antifreeze inaccessible, as well as pesticides, cleaning products, painting and art supplies, gardening sprays and pellets, lubricants, and other harmful poisons. Clean up all of these and store them in closed sheds, drawers, or cabinets that the puppy can't access, not even with a prying nose and paws.

Garden

Review the exhaustive list from the ASPCA (see Resources) on plants to avoid having in your yard. Also switch to the use of lawn care and pesticide products that are explicitly safe for pets.

Outdoor Living Spaces

If your puppy will be spending unaccompanied stretches of time outdoors, you will need to consider which items might attract chewing. Lawn furniture can be very alluring. Exposed drip irrigation lines are also like a fun puzzle to your puppy; no matter how much they dig and pull up, there's always more. Water hoses, pool equipment, sports equipment, mulch, and small pebbles are all items your puppy might enjoy chewing. Tidy your yard with this in mind before you leave your puppy unattended, or purchase an outdoor kennel to safely contain them.

PREVENT BOLTING

If you or someone in your household leaves the door open, your puppy will bolt outside. This is an expression of their natural curiosity and need to explore. But if they bolt, they are headed for danger. There's no need to install any special devices, but you do need to ensure that everyone in your household, including visitors, are acutely aware of the importance of not leaving doors ajar. Use puppy gates and pens to further keep your puppy safely contained in a confined area within your home. Make sure gates are secure at all times; don't assume all visitors will close the gate on the way out. Make sure all fencing is in good order with no weak boards or gaps. You'd be amazed at how small a space a puppy can squeeze through. I have an enormous 100-pound dog; you should have seen my jaw drop the first time I saw him climb through the teeny-tiny square window at the back of my pickup truck's cab. It was like watching a magician perform an impossible trick. And remember, some dogs can dig and will dig right under your fence. Keep your puppy supervised, and if they're a digger, you'll need fence posts that go far enough down into the ground if you're planning on sometimes leaving them alone in the yard when they're older.

Reduce Risks of Infection

Many people assume that diseases are spread from a sick dog to a not-yet-fully-vaccinated dog like your puppy, but this isn't the case. All pets, even healthy and fully vaccinated ones, should be viewed as potential carriers of serious diseases that could jeopardize the health of your puppy when they are less than 16 weeks old. The reason is simple: a healthy vaccinated dog may frequent the dog park, attend doggy day care, or even meet other dogs when out on a walk and pick up germs on their coat, paws, and muzzle that can then be transmitted to your puppy.

And it's not only healthy adult pets to be wary of; this includes you, too. While you were out walking around the city today, you picked up who knows what on the soles of your shoes. When you have a puppy aged less than 16 weeks, get in the habit of removing your shoes whenever you get home and stash them out of your puppy's reach. Better safe than sorry.

Besides removing shoes, limit your puppy's exposure to any pets who frequent dog parks or dog day care. You can learn more about this topic in Socializing Your Puppy.

Supervise Kids

It's hard to imagine anything more adorable than a child and a puppy cuddling together, but the truth is that puppies and kids aren't an ideal combination. If you do have young children, special care must be taken. The reason is that puppies will view small children more as other puppies (competing for their resources) than as human beings like yourself. Simply put, your puppy *can* harm a child or a child *can* unintentionally harm your puppy.

Always supervise child and puppy interactions. That's rule #1. They should never be alone together because accidents happen in a flash. When you begin Loose Leash Walking, don't include your child. They can too easily be pulled down to the ground by a vivacious puppy. And children are likely to pull on the leash, harming your training efforts.

Lastly, one more tip for you (besides never leaving them unattended). In The Six Key Commands, you're going to learn all about positive reinforcement and using rewards to cement positive associations. Use these techniques to teach your puppy that kids are awesome. When your child is near, give the puppy a treat. *You* should give the puppy the treat, not the child, because you're still working on developing safety and trust between puppy and child. Work up to the child giving your puppy a treat later, once you've witnessed that your puppy isn't at all anxious when the child approaches.

Puppy Rules for Kids

Teach any children who will interact with your puppy the following rules.

- Leave the puppy alone when they are eating.
- Don't take away a toy the puppy is playing with.
- Let sleeping puppies lie, including staying away from their crate when they're inside napping.
- Don't try to ride or pick up the puppy.
- Don't put your face right up to the puppy's face; this isn't how puppies greet each other.
- Gentle petting is wonderful, but no hugs; puppies may look like they want to be hugged, but they don't.
- Do not pull the puppy's tail, stick your fingers in their mouth or ears, or touch their paws; all of these things are uncomfortable or unnerving for a puppy.

When to Visit the Vet

REGULARLY SCHEDULED VISITS

The average age of a puppy when you bring them home is about eight weeks. If they've already had a vet visit—which is likely—be sure to get all the paperwork so you can give it to your own veterinarian. You should plan your first visit to the vet with your puppy shortly after their arrival, ideally within one week. Important to keep in mind: depending on where you got your puppy, be sure to read the agreement. Some breeders and some rescue organizations have an absolute requirement that you take the puppy to the vet within a specifically prescribed time interval.

Your puppy's first round of "vaccinations" came from their mother in the form of antibodies in her milk. That's powerful stuff, but it only lasts so long. Your puppy will require three rounds (some vets may recommend four) of vaccinations from a veterinarian in order to build up a safe level of immunity to distemper, hepatitis, parvo, parainfluenza (those four are given in combination as DHPP), and rabies. Your veterinarian may also recommend additional vaccinations such as Bordetella or kennel cough, and others based on the region in which you live.

Typically, the three stages of vaccinations will occur at the ages of six to eight weeks, 10 to 12 weeks, and at 16 weeks. At that point, your puppy is considered fully vaccinated but will require additional boosters every year or three years, depending on the vaccine. Your veterinarian's office will give you more information about this, and more than likely will send out helpful reminders via postcard, e-mail, or text message.

During each of these visits, your vet will also do puppy wellness checks, examining their weight and vitals, a stool sample, and their coat. Your vet will be looking for any sign of parasites in their stool, fleas and ticks in their coat, and a healthy weight, among other items on the vet's wellness checklist.

If you don't plan to breed your dog, you should also discuss neutering (male) or spaying (female) with your veterinarian to learn their recommendations with regard to timing for the procedure.

EMERGENCIES

If you know that your dog has ingested something poisonous, seek out a vet immediately. The same goes for a serious injury, like being hit by a car or choking (see here). Here are some additional signs that might warrant an unscheduled trip to the vet:

- **Allergies:** Dogs have allergies, just as we do, and this will typically manifest by your puppy excessively licking, chewing, and scratching themselves. These are normal dog activities, so only be concerned if they seem excessive or if the puppy has red, irritated skin or a rash.

- **Vomit or diarrhea:** If either happens once or twice, then goes away, don't fret. But if your puppy is regularly exhibiting either symptom, take them to the vet.

- **Limp:** A limp lasting longer than a day or two, or that recurs, should be examined by a veterinarian right away.

- **Lump:** While there are many benign causes of lumps, there are also very serious malignant ones, so if you see or feel a lump, take your puppy to your vet.

- **Excessive drinking:** This can be an early sign of diabetes, so it is best to take your puppy to the vet right away for the appropriate tests to be run.

part two

The Training Steps

Learning happens. Training is intentional. Your puppy has been learning every moment of every day since they were born. Training means taking the reins and deciding what lessons you want your puppy to learn. It means being vigilant and rewarding all desirable behaviors. And it means having restraint: ignoring or redirecting all undesirable behaviors in order to extinguish them. Training requires intentionality, consistency, and clarity. It means, for example, always using the same one word and not confusing your puppy with multiple commands for the same thing.

Even when you're not actively training, your puppy is still learning. Your puppy is watching you and learning from you all the time.

In this section, we'll share with you our seven steps of puppy training. All are deeply rooted in the practice of positive reinforcement. Throughout, we'll shed light on how puppies perceive the world, and we'll offer tips for success. We'll cover everything from their first days in your home, to their bodily needs—eating, sleeping, and elimination—to their social, mental, and emotional requirements. Let's get started.

STEP 1

bringing your puppy home

The day you bring your puppy home, and likely for a few days after, one feeling will dominate your puppy's experience: stress. Regardless of the surfeit of love, attention, cuddling, and coziness you're about to bestow upon them, anything and everything they experience is likely to be stressful, because change causes stress. Everything is about to change for them. A new place, new people, new smells, and the spotlight of attention.

It's true that some puppies make this transition easily and with minimal stress. If this happens, great. But err on the side of assuming that introducing your puppy to their new home will be very stressful. Give them three full days to adjust, three days in which you will cater to eliminating as much stress as possible.

Puppy Perspective

Your puppy's earliest memories are of their mother and siblings. To you, they're beyond special. But back then, they were one of several littermates and not the center of attention. They were confined to a small area and never given the run of the place, so recognize that this state is their comfort zone. Your puppy feels much more comfortable in smaller spaces.

Back in that penned-in area, only safe objects were permitted by the breeder, rescue, or shelter. Spurred by the innate drive to put their mouth on everything, they developed the notion that they can chew on anything and everything.

While their mother was probably not around, since puppies are separated from the mother during weaning, your puppy's earliest days were likely spent roughhousing with their siblings, jumping on their backs, tackling, and being tackled. It is this puppy who will be entering your home, expecting that everything is fair game when it comes to chewing, pawing, knocking around, and jumping. Things are about to get interesting.

Before You Bring Puppy Home

To make puppy's first day in your home as stress-free as possible, be sure to prep in advance.

Get everything in order: Go shopping. Prepare your home. Buy all your supplies (see Puppy Supplies Checklist) ahead of time, and get your home in order (see Puppy-Proof Your Home), because when you bring your puppy home your job is to eliminate stress.

Plan to go directly home: We've seen too many first-time puppy owners who stop at a pet supply store on the way home. Stops add unnecessary stress for your pup, so plan ahead. The same applies to stopping to visit your friends and relatives on the drive home to show off your adorable new pup. It's so tempting, but resist the urge. You need to go directly home. Let everyone know they can meet the puppy in a few days. They'll understand.

Collar and tag: When you get your puppy, they will either have no collar or likely a light ribbon or temporary collar. Remove any temporary collar and put on the collar you bought for them, with the I.D. tag already attached. It should be loose enough that you can fit a couple of fingers between your puppy and the collar, but not so loose it hangs like a necklace. They will probably be confused and scratch at it. Just ignore this. They'll get used to it very soon. Expect for them to be confused and annoyed by it initially.

Borrow some food: Before heading out to pick up your puppy, find out what kind of food they've been eating. You may have selected a different food, so you should prepare for this transition. If they've been eating something different, ask if it would be possible for the breeder, rescue, or shelter to give you a small portion. If they won't, consider purchasing a small bag of the old food. During the course of the puppy's first week in your home, mix a bit of the new food in with the old food. Each day, add more of the new food and less of the old food until after about a week they have fully transitioned to the new food. Refer to Puppy Supplies Checklist, for more information on adding variety to your dog's diet.

Bringing Puppy Home

These simple steps will ensure that your puppy is calm and safe on the ride home and that your car stays relatively clean.

Crate or harness: If your puppy's crate is small enough to fit in your vehicle, you should anchor it with a strap. If the crate won't fit, we recommend purchasing a safety harness for your puppy's ride home. It's not safe to drive with your puppy in your lap.

Bring a friend: If it's at all possible, bring a second person with you when you pick up your puppy. One person needs to do the driving. The other should sit beside the puppy and pet them and speak to them reassuringly to help alleviate stress. Most puppies have never been in a car before.

Prepare your car: Cover your car seats with towels. It's safe to assume your puppy will throw up during the drive. Bring extra towels to help with cleaning them and the car during the drive. Diarrhea is also possible, though less likely. Stress and motion sickness can cause both vomiting and diarrhea, and your puppy may also pee in the car.

Skip the treats: Some people ask us if they should bring treats to reward their puppy on the drive home, to teach them positive associations with being in the car. It's a good impulse, and eventually yes, you will want to reinforce this. But not today.

Today just get them home. They're too nervous to enjoy the treats and might throw them up. The next few days are not a time for training, just adjustment.

For long drives: If it's going to be a long drive, bring food, water, poop bags, extra towels, collar, and leash. If your drive is longer than one hour, plan a break at the halfway point to take them out to potty, drink, and, if they'll eat, have a snack.

Arriving home: When you get home, carry your puppy inside either in their crate or in your arms. Your mission for the next few days is to keep everything as calm and peaceful as possible.

Showing Your Puppy Around

When you walk in the door, there's no need to show your puppy around (this is your crate, here's my bedroom, this is where we keep the paper towels). You're not a bed-and-breakfast host. You should be doing these things instead:

Go potty: Go directly to their designated potty area. We will go over this more in Potty Training. This might be out in your yard or inside where you've laid down puppy pads on the floor. Hang out with them until they've relieved themselves.

Hydrate: Next, take them to the area you've selected for their water dish. Let them take a drink.

Hang out: Lastly, enjoy your first hangout session with your pup. Select a confined area by closing doors or using puppy gates or a playpen. Think back to their time with their mother and stick to a limited space. Sit on the floor and chat and interact if your puppy needs to burn off a bit of energy. Remember they're disoriented, lonely, and confused, so your love and attention are really valuable. And if you have other members of your household, this is a fine time for them to come say hello, too. Your puppy should meet all of their new family on day one.

Nap: Your hangout session isn't likely to last for long. They probably need a nap. You'll see their eyes getting drowsy or they may just lie down. Puppies need 16 to 20 hours of sleep a day. That's right. You may have big plans for your puppy, but actual awake and alert time is incredibly limited. Wherever they drop, just let them nap there and leave them be. They're exhausted.

Signs of Stress

Bringing your puppy home will begin a long process of introducing them to people and situations. You never want to force your puppy into any interaction if they are uncomfortable or stressed out. If they are stressed, end the interaction at once and take your puppy to a safe space. The key is recognizing *when* they are stressed. Here's a list of some key signs of stress, and also see **Resources** for a link to a visual guide to dog body language.

- Pulling away
- Whining
- Tail between legs
- Trembling
- Hiding under or behind something or someone
- Ears hanging very low
- "Half-moon eyes" where your puppy looks sideways and you can see the white of their eyes

Introductions to Adults

These do's and don'ts are tips for you and all members of your household, but also advice to share with the friends and relatives who will flock over to meet your puppy after their first few restful days at home.

Do's and Don'ts

- **Do** sit on the ground or as low as physically possible.
- **Don't** loom over them from above.
- For men, **do** raise the pitch of your voice so it doesn't sound too growly.
- **Don't** force any interaction if your puppy shows signs of stress (see here).
- **Do** see if your puppy will take treats from the open hand of someone seated on the ground, especially if the puppy has seemed wary of them.

Introductions to Kids

See Puppy Rules for Kids for our recommendations about how young children should be taught to interact with your new puppy. Remember to reward your puppy when the kids are near. Monitoring and supervision are key. Until you are 100 percent sure that your kids are with the program, never leave them alone with the puppy.

> → Tip: Positive reinforcement works just as well on kids as it does on puppies. When you see that your child is following the rules for interacting with the puppy, give your kid tons of praise and positive feedback.

Introduction to Your (Older) Dog

While we'll cover socializing your puppy with dogs and other pets in more detail in Socializing Your Puppy, if you already have a dog in the home, the rules are a bit different. For example, normally you'd seek out a neutral territory, but there is no neutral space in your home; it all "belongs" to your older dog, and you're not going to drive out to a park on your puppy's first day.

As with the rest of your family, your puppy and older dog do need to meet on day one. There's no avoiding it, even though it may cause some stress. And so, if you already have a dog, here are some simple tips to foster a positive first meet and greet.

Wait and sequester: While this meeting needs to happen on day one, it shouldn't occur right when your puppy first walks in the door. Get them situated first. Prior to heading out to pick up your puppy, you should put away all of your older dog's resources (toys, chews, etc.) to prevent territorial disputes. Sequester your dog in another room before you head out so the puppy isn't overwhelmed when they first arrive.

Keep it brief: Don't put your puppy on a leash, since they probably have never worn one before and this could add stress. You might want to put your older dog on a leash; trust that you'll know best. When you introduce your puppy to their new big brother or sister, let them interact for just a minute or two, then separate them. If the two seem happy together and it's going well, let them meet again—your puppy might find a familiar comfort in being around another dog. If it's not going well, you may need the help of a trainer.

Puppy manners (or lack thereof): In dog language, a puppy's greetings would be viewed as rather rude and inappropriate, a bit like a perfect stranger running up to you on the street and hugging you. The good news is that your older dog recognizes that your puppy is a puppy and will typically give them a "puppy pass." That's how we refer to the forbearance older dogs tend to show puppies.

After the honeymoon: Sadly, a puppy pass only goes so far. At some point, when your puppy is around four months of age, your older dog will begin to tell them off with a growl, nip, or swat. This is normal and a perfectly good lesson for your puppy to learn about boundaries and how to politely interact with adult dogs.

Manage your older dog's stress level: The introduction of the new puppy is going to be stressful for your dog. Look for signs such as raised hackles, growling, or a stiff tail. Give your older dog plenty of breaks from being around the puppy, and also show your dog lots of extra attention. Resources such as toys and food are typically the most likely cause of conflict, so be sure to separate your older dog and puppy around such resources. Your affectionate attention is absolutely another powerful resource, so take care to provide separate attention to each.

Peace crate: In Crate Training, we'll cover crate training. For now, you should know that once your puppy is all set up in their new crate, this will restore order to your home. The crate is the most effective way to reduce the stress load on your older dog.

Meet Your Puppy: Some Behaviors to Keep in Mind

So far, we've discussed how to introduce your puppy to the creatures, spaces, and objects in their new home. But introductions go both ways. One of the most important goals of this book is helping *you* get to know and understand your new family member. This is especially true if this is your first time raising a puppy. The day you bring them home, you will likely have a few very specific worries on your mind. The reputation of puppies precedes them, and this includes jumping up, destructive chewing, nipping, and excessive barking.

JUMPING UP

We'll cover this topic in much more detail in The Six Key Commands with the *Off* command, but for now it's useful to understand how this problem typically originates.

Think ahead: Yes, a little puppy jumping up and wagging their tail is adorable. Who can resist the urge to lean down and play? *You* can resist this urge, and you *need* to resist this urge. Because the puppy who learns this is a fine thing to do will in the blink of an eye become a 100-pound dog who tackles your guests or a 10-

pound dog who scratches people's legs. Good habits start young.

Negative equals positive: Your puppy adores attention and does not distinguish between positive and negative attention. So, if they jump up and you push them down, that was a fun little game—you just rewarded them.

The opposite of reward: A fallacy held by many puppy owners is the belief that the opposite of reward is punishment. It is not.

The opposite of reward is no reward.

It's taking your ball and going home. The consequence for a jumping puppy should be: absolutely nothing. The consequence for a puppy who is sitting, lying down, or busy with a toy when someone walks in the door (i.e., anything other than jumping up) should be: praise, petting, love, and attention.

Reward the behaviors you want. Ignore or redirect the behaviors you don't.

DESTRUCTIVE CHEWING

Puppies go through a teething stage during which they feel the irresistible urge to chew on everything in your home. It is a normal behavior for young pups and may become quite intense around teething time, especially around four to five months old.

Chewing is essential: It helps maintain the health of your dog's teeth, jaws, and gums. The drive is so strong that when your puppy encounters any and all objects in your home, they view them through the lens of "Can I chew it?"

You choose what they chew: Your job is to answer your puppy's question by letting them know what they can chew and what they can't. Chew toys, for example, are the perfect target to redirect their chewing needs. Not all puppies are drawn instinctively to chew on a toy—that table leg and that electrical cord can seem much more enticing—so you may need to reinforce that behavior by giving your puppy treats every time they are given a chew toy. You can also stuff many chew toys with treats; see our comments about puzzle toys and using them for feeding (here). Use chew toys stuffed with or paired with treats as a frequent reward to further reinforce your preference that they choose chew toys.

Never punish: If you scold or otherwise punish your puppy for chewing on the wrong thing, this is bad for your relationship, and it will backfire. Punishment will simply encourage your puppy to chew when you are not around, as they will have learned that you are the source of punishment and will avoid this by not chewing in front of you. Instead of punishing, redirect your puppy's chew drive to a toy and praise, praise, praise.

NIPPING

As we've seen with chewing, puppies are mouthy creatures, and their oral fixation will extend to your own body; fingers, toes, ankles, nose, and earlobes are especially alluring.

Boundaries: In the section on introducing your puppy to an older dog, we talked about the puppy pass and how it only extends so far. A similar rule applies to you and your puppy. There's nothing wrong with your puppy gently nibbling at your fingers for the first few weeks. But you don't need to put up with pain. If your puppy is nipping too hard, they need to learn where to draw the line.

Ouch!: Your puppy should be playing with toys, not your body. If they nip your hands or arms instead of the toy, simply pull your hand away and say, "Ouch!" and redirect them back to the toy and praise them as they chew it instead of you. If they continue to try to bite you instead of the toy, say, "Ouch!" again, withdraw your hand, and remove yourself from playtime. Ignore your puppy. Go check your e-mail. Your puppy will learn that biting you instead of toys results in the end of playtime altogether, which is not what they want.

Don't punish or overreact: Note that we said to *say* ouch, not to yell at your puppy. Never use shouting or physical punishment, as this can damage your relationship, cause mistrust, and sow the seeds for behavioral issues down the road. After all, your puppy didn't do anything *wrong*; they are doing what comes naturally and need to learn.

EXCESSIVE BARKING

Dogs bark. It is a natural part of their communication and behavior. We presume you're okay with some barking or else you wouldn't have invited a puppy to share your home. Some breeds do far more alert barking than others. Most dogs will bark when someone is at your door or when they hear a strange, loud noise such as a car backfiring.

Intruder alert: We hope you'll agree that it's a good thing for your puppy to bark when someone tries to get into your home; this includes knocking on the door or ringing the bell. Being a burglar alarm is a great job for your puppy as long as they don't sit at the door or window and bark at every passerby.

Exit barking: Adult dogs don't normally bark when you leave home; if they do, this is usually a symptom of separation anxiety. For puppies, on the other hand, exit barking or whining is a fairly common occurrence. The last thing you want to do is spend your day worrying if your puppy is still at it, causing your puppy undue stress and potentially irritating your neighbors. The best way to handle this is a combination of redirection, distraction, and a stealthy exit. The night before, moisten your dog's breakfast kibble and squeeze this goo plus a couple of treats into a stuffable toy and pop it in the freezer. In the morning, hand the frozen toy to your pup. This is like breakfast and a crossword puzzle all in one: it's going to take them a long, long time of deeply focused chewing to extricate their meal. Alternatively, you can use a long-lasting chew such as a bully stick or tendon. While they're otherwise engaged, off you go, without fanfare. This will greatly mitigate or even eliminate exit barking.

Nuisance barking: If you're home and your puppy is just barking and barking to get your attention, you should extinguish this behavior. We extinguish behaviors by not reacting to them at all. No reward, no attention. When they're quiet, on the other hand, heap on the praise. The first time your puppy ever barks for your attention, they're putting out feelers to see if this will succeed. If you give in and play with them, tell them to be quiet, yell at them to shut up, pet them to calm them down, or anything at all other than ignore them, you've just rewarded this behavior. Notice that that list included reactions that are both nice and not so nice. It doesn't matter. They've found a button they can push, and now they'll keep on pushing it. Instead, *do nothing*. You can even turn your back and leave the room. That isn't at all what they wanted. Don't give in. Eventually they'll stop. And when they stop . . . *that* is when you walk over and pet, praise, and reward them. Remember, if you're going about your day and your puppy is lying there peacefully, take a moment to praise and reinforce this calm behavior.

Introduction to Healthy Habits

Grooming is important for your dog's health and physical comfort. It's also a great way for you to bond with your puppy. Puppies don't generally enjoy having their paws, mouth, or ears handled, so it's best to help them get used to the physicality of grooming at an early age, and with plenty of positive reinforcement. This helps with vet and groomer visits, too, so your puppy can remain calm when these professionals are handling them.

Dental care: As your ankles or arms can attest, puppy teeth are sharp. At around 16 weeks, your puppy will begin to lose their puppy teeth as the adult teeth grow in. You might see some bleeding from the gums or blood on their toys—this is normal. Even before their adult teeth have grown in, this is a perfect time to get them used to having their teeth brushed. There are products such as a powder you can add to your puppy's food or water that keeps teeth clean systemically by interacting with saliva, but nothing works better than a toothbrush and toothpaste. There are many different types of toothbrushes for dogs, but at this age just getting them used to having something in their mouth is a positive first step. If their puppy teeth are loose, be extra gentle. You can ask your vet, a groomer, or trainer to show you how to effectively brush your puppy's teeth.

Puppy pedicures: Get your puppy used to having their nails handled from an early age and you will avoid future frustration. File gently with a nail file or simply hold each nail between your thumb and forefinger to accustom your puppy to the sensation. Give your puppy treats as you hold their nails in your hand, to make this into a rewarding activity. A puppy who holds still for nail trimming is far less likely to get nicked by a clipper. If you haven't done this before, ask your vet, a groomer, or a trainer to show you how, as dogs have a blood vessel that runs through the nail, and trimming their nails improperly can cause bleeding. A product we recommend is styptic powder for dogs. If you do nick that vessel, simply apply the powder to stop the bleeding and start the healing.

Ear care: Check your puppy's ears frequently for dirt or signs of infection. While ear infections are common in all dogs, some breeds are more prone to them than others. Wipe out the outer ear canal regularly using a cotton ball and a mild ear cleanser. Take breaks to give your puppy a treat. If you have a puppy with a long, fleecy coat, fur will often grow down into the ear canal and will need to be plucked—let a groomer or your vet do this for you.

Bathing and brushing: Unless your puppy is really filthy, you don't need to bathe them every week, as this will strip the natural oils from their skin and coat. However, you should get your puppy used to having their coat brushed at least once a week. For long-coated dogs, this will prevent tangles and matting. For short-coated dogs, it will reduce shedding. Make sure you purchase the right type of brush for your puppy's coat. Most puppies really enjoy being brushed, so the act of gentle brushing is often reward enough. But if your puppy is squeamish, take plenty of breaks and be generous with the treats.

STEP 2

crate training

People who have never owned a dog before sometimes make the mistake of equating a crate with a jail cell and wonder why you'd punish a little puppy by sticking them in jail. But this has it all backward. From the puppy's point of view, going to the crate is much more like a retreat to a cozy inn. It's a place of tranquility, warmth, and comfort.

The term we like to use for crate training is "thoughtful confinement." The crate will serve as your puppy's home within your home.

Puppy Perspective

Did you ever wonder why dogs are so drawn to hanging out under tables, under the bed, and in other little hidey-holes? It's because dogs are den animals. They love to feel protected inside a shelter. A puppy therefore views a crate as a den.

Puppies also view their crate primarily as their bedroom. And they were born with a deep drive to avoid soiling their sleeping quarters.

While we hope we've made it clear that you should view the crate as your puppy does—a cozy little den—that doesn't mean they want to spend all day in there. It's a happy safe space, but your home has plenty of other places they should enjoy exploring (supervised, of course) throughout the day.

Benefits of Crate Training

This cozy hub will provide several key benefits:

- The crate is essential in potty training. We'll cover this in much more detail in the next chapter. For now, it's helpful to understand that crate training and potty training intersect at the point of a puppy's born instinct not to go to the bathroom where they sleep.

- The crate prevents myriad minor and major disasters in your home by restricting your puppy's access to roam around and chew the place to shreds.

- The crate will serve as a time clock, where your puppy punches in and out to mark the events of its day.

Your job is to help imbue the crate with an aura of joy and welcoming warmth so your puppy will truly enjoy this thoughtful confinement.

What Kind of Crate?

We covered this in Puppy Supplies Checklist, but just as a reminder, purchase a crate that will fit your puppy when they're all grown up. For very small breeds, this is straightforward. For everyone else, it means your crate will come with dividers that you will reposition as your puppy grows.

The crate size and/or position of dividers should always give your puppy just enough room to comfortably turn around and lie down, and no more than that. A too-big crate is a primary cause of potty-training issues.

Outfitting the Crate

Since your puppy's crate is a stand-in for their den, you'll want to make it as cozy and inviting as possible. Here are the ways to achieve maximum comfort for your pup:

Your scent: As we mentioned in the Puppy Supplies Checklist, don't purchase any kind of expensive dog bed or mat for the crate, as your puppy will destroy it. Use old towels. Or (a favorite tip) use your old T-shirts, as your scent will provide a wonderful comfort.

Mom's scent: Another tip is when you pick up your puppy, ask if you can have some of their old bedding, perhaps an old blanket or towel that they used with their mother and littermates. A treasured plush toy will work as well. Most breeders, shelters, and rescues will oblige this request. This, too, can provide reassurance and comfort.

Heartbeat: Many people like to include the element of sound. A white noise generator placed next to the crate can help mask new and possibly frightening sounds. Some white noise generators have a heartbeat sound that can remind your puppy of their mother. You can also go old school by taking a low-tech clock that audibly ticks, wrapping it in a muffling towel, and sticking it in a corner of the crate. It's unlikely your puppy will try to get at the clock and chew it due to their sleep patterns and because it's so soothing. However, if you do hear them messing with the clock, you can remove it.

Keep it clean: Everything (other than the clock) that you put in the crate should be machine washable or disposable. Help your puppy with hygiene by washing the bedding about once a week. Yes, that means you'll be washing out the scent of their mother and littermates, but it's okay; that bedding served a useful purpose during your puppy's first days in their new home, when it was needed most.

Reduce sensory overload: It is also useful to have a large sheet or something similar to drape over the entire crate to cut down on light. This doesn't just make it easier for them to sleep in there because it's darker; it also thoughtfully confines their eyeballs. Without the drape, they will be far too curious about watching all the goings-on. For just that reason, you should feel free to use the sheet during the daytime as well, when they're down for a nap inside the crate. A sheet reduces sensory overload.

Where to Locate the Crate

Dogs want to be where you are, so it's important to locate their crate with that in mind.

Follow the action: While you are crate training, the crate should be located wherever you happen to be. It doesn't have to remain in a fixed location. This means that at nighttime, you should place the crate in your bedroom, as close to your bedside as possible. And during the day, if you are primarily hanging out in the living room, move the crate there. If you purchased an enormous crate due to your puppy's future size, dragging that thing around could pose a challenge. For you, we'd recommend purchasing an inexpensive small crate to use during these first few weeks at home.

Share your bedroom: Once they are fully potty trained, you can establish a permanent spot for the crate in your home or you can continue to move it around. We recommend that the crate remains in your bedroom or that of any other family member at night. If you plan to eventually eliminate the crate, we would still suggest that just as your puppy slept in your bedroom inside their crate during crate training, once they are grown you should continue to let them sleep in your bedroom at night, minus the crate. This acknowledges and celebrates your dog's identity as a den animal and will provide them ongoing comfort. Dogs naturally sleep in a pile, so even if they're not literally sharing your bed, just sharing this den at night enhances bonding between you and your pup.

If you're already wondering when you can ditch the crate, skip ahead to Transitioning Out of the Crate.

Traveling with a Crate

If you're going to take your puppy on vacation with you, their crate is a perfect way to bring a piece of home with you. Rather than leaving your puppy in the hotel room or rental home with free run of the place, they should stay in their crate. It helps to reinforce potty and sleeping schedules, too.

Some people like to purchase lightweight fabric or canvas crates just for travel. This may be fine for an adult dog, but we strongly advise against them for puppies. Puppies may chew them to pieces.

How to Crate Train Your Puppy

Crate training typically happens pretty quickly. It may take a few weeks, but it's not at all unheard of to successfully crate train in a mere matter of days. Here's the program:

STEP 1: INTRODUCE YOUR PUPPY TO THE CRATE

Sprinkle some treats: Set up the crate in your living room. Drop some treats inside the crate to encourage exploration. Be careful not to let the door swing closed by accident and surprise your puppy.

Don't force it: If your puppy is wary of entering the crate, don't force it. Keep adding more treats farther back, closer to the rear wall. You can add toys, too. Eventually your puppy will go inside to get the treats or toy.

Make the crate magic: Keep the crate door open throughout the day, and from time to time, when your puppy isn't looking, toss some treats into the crate for them to discover. It's very important that they do not catch you doing this. The idea is that *you* are not the one giving them the treats. It's that magical crate in which treats materialize. This is an extremely effective technique you should keep up throughout the day, for several days. They're going to love that magical crate.

STEP 2: FEED INSIDE THE CRATE WITH THE DOOR OPEN

Place their meal in back: For their first meal, place the food dish all the way to the rear of the crate. They should enter and dine.

Leave the door open.

If needed, place their meal in front: If they are reluctant to enter, put their food dish inside near the entryway so they are simply sticking their head inside to eat. This is a fine first step.

Inch the bowl back: During the following meals, keep nudging the bowl closer to the far wall until finally they will fully enter to eat. Remember that *hunger is your ally.* If they're hungry, they're going to be extremely motivated to go inside and dine.

Their water dish never goes inside the crate, but if you'd like to move it nearer to the outside of the crate, that's fine.

Only move on to Step 3 once they fully enter the crate to eat their meal. If you're unable to complete Step 2 because your puppy is terrified of the crate, this reflects some adverse experience they had before you brought them home or a genetic predisposition toward fear; seek the help of a professional trainer.

STEP 3: FEED INSIDE THE CRATE WITH THE DOOR CLOSED

In they go: Place their dinner by the crate's rear wall. When they enter to eat, close the door. Hang out nearby to keep them company while they eat.

Out they go: The moment they finish eating, open the door and let them out. Don't wait for any special overture from them that they want to come out. You're there at the ready, attentively opening the door as soon as they have eaten all their food.

STEP 4: SHORT STINTS

One minute: After they're fine eating their meal inside with the door closed, for their next meal leave them inside for a full minute after they finish before opening the door.

Build to 10 minutes: At the following meal, move on to a few minutes, and keep increasing the duration until they can wait 10 minutes inside the crate with the door closed before you release them.

Always wait for quiet: *This is crucial.* If your puppy is inside the crate and whining to come out or go potty, do not let them out until they stop whining or barking. Simply stand there and wait until they stop. This might take a minute. It could take up to 10 minutes. But at some point—even if just for a moment—they will stop, and *that* is when you open the door. Immediately. It's so important that you maintain this kind of attentiveness while you are crate training. Bad habits are born the moment you open the door while they are still whining. By whining, they are simply trying out Plan A for getting out. We want them to realize that Plan A never works whereas Plan B, silence, works every time. Do not scold them or tap on the crate. Such acts of frustration will, at best, make crate training take a lot longer. At worst, your puppy could become terrified of the crate and of you.

STEP 5: LONGER DURATIONS

Use the crate command sequence: Once they have mastered 10 minutes, you're ready to teach them the command Crate. Call them over. Show them the treat you have in your hand. Say Crate as you toss the treat inside. The moment they enter the crate, say the verbal marker Yes and allow them to enjoy their reward inside the crate after you close the door. You'll learn more about verbal markers in The Six Key Commands. Praise them warmly and affectionately for what a great job they've done.

Exit to another room: Now take your exit and retire to another room of your home for 10 to 15 minutes.

Minimize distractions: While you're in the other room, don't talk on the phone, as your voice will be too much of a distraction. During these stretches, have any other members of your household collaborate by keeping noise to a minimum. No kids running past the crate. It's okay to have the TV on; a television is like white noise to a puppy.

Retrieve them: As long as they're quiet, head back and let them out of the crate and reward them with praise and some playtime. If they're whining or barking, wait for them to stop before you let them out.

Anticipate: It may take you a couple of days to develop this skill, but you can often listen closely from the other room and anticipate that your puppy is *about* to whine before they actually do. Listen for sounds of restlessness: pawing at the door or walking around in circles. If you hear this, head back early and let them out before the whining begins.

Repeat: You should repeat this step several times each day and not just during mealtimes. Each time, try to remain in the other room for longer stretches of time until you hit 30 minutes. Once you hit 30 minutes, you're ready for Step 6. Don't be surprised if you reach Step 6 after only a few days.

STEP 6: LEAVING THE HOUSE

Pick a challenging treat: This is going to be extremely similar to Step 5, but you're going to want to select a long-lasting treat. A tendon, a natural chew, a puzzle toy full of treats, or a stuffable chew toy that you've filled with food and frozen (see Exit Barking) are all good options that will occupy their attention for 10 to 15 minutes. Toys are fine, too, such as a hard ball (not a tennis ball). You're going to be leaving them alone with this treat or toy, so remember you should have previously screened your puppy by watching them interact with these same items while under your supervision. See Separation Anxiety to understand why you're providing them with this long-lasting treat.

Use the command sequence: Show the treat. Say Crate as you toss in the special treat. Say Yes when they enter. Close the door and praise.

Putter: Don't leave the house immediately. Fix your hair or read something funny your friend just posted online. Stall for a couple of minutes before you leave. Why? Because if you always put your puppy in the crate and then immediately exit, your puppy will associate the crate with you leaving. We want to avoid all negative associations with the crate.

Leave the house: Exit without fanfare, and stay away for 30 minutes, to mirror the 30-minute duration they've already mastered in Step 5.

STEP 7: RETURNING HOME

Return matter-of-factly: Come back inside, set down your keys, get a drink of water, then in a very low-key manner mosey over to let your puppy out of the crate. If your puppy is super excited to see you, resist the urge to find this flattering and reward it. Getting so excited after a short separation is irrational—you have not just returned from war, you were only away for half an hour—so don't reinforce it. Even if it's eating you up on the inside and you just want to run over and give your puppy a great big hug, resist. If you make a beeline for the crate and match your puppy's enthusiasm, separation anxiety is born. See Separation Anxiety for more.

Let them out: Remember not to let them out of their crate if they are barking or whining. Return to the same practice you did before: wait patiently for them to be quiet and only then open the crate door and give them a mild greeting.

STEP 8: OVERNIGHT CRATING

We will cover this topic in additional detail in Potty Training.

Crate placement: The crate should be next to your bed for the first several nights. This helps you be more immediately aware of their potty needs. Just as importantly, it reduces their social isolation by embracing your puppy's existence as a den animal. You two are sharing a den.

Command sequence: Call your puppy, show the treat, say *Crate* and toss in the treat, close the door after they enter, and praise them. Cover the crate with a sheet or similar draping fabric.

Keep calm: From the moment you cover the crate, you should refrain from talking to your puppy. As the night goes on, they may whine because they are lonely and still transitioning to their new life. If they're whining, neither shush nor reassure verbally. Simply reach your hand down near the crate so they can smell you. If this calms them down, they were feeling lonely. If the whining persists, they probably need to potty. See *Potty Training* for more information.

Puppy's First Night

One of the most common questions we're asked is about puppy's very first night home. In this chapter and in **Potty Training** are instructions for your puppy sleeping in their crate overnight, but on their first night they aren't yet crate trained at all. Isn't this an impossible contradiction?

Why yes, it is. This answer is far from ideal, but it's based in reality. Simply know that the first night will probably be rough. Your puppy likely does have some crate experience from before (breeders, foster families, shelters, and rescues are likely to have used a crate), but your puppy may not yet be quite ready to sleep overnight in the crate. Nonetheless, the two of you need to do it anyway.

It should comfort you to know that your puppy's first day likely exhausted them; they also have a natural inclination to sleep at night, and they will be craving a small, enclosed den. All of these factors work in your favor.

The best you can do is work on crate training as much as you can during their first day then hope for the best. And maybe plan on not operating any heavy machinery the next morning. It's going to be a challenging night . . .

The reason you provide your puppy with a long-lasting snack, puzzle, or toy before you leave the house is to keep them occupied for 10 to 15 minutes. It's during this time that you will exit the house, an event that otherwise would be likely to cause them stress. Because they're so focused on their treat, they don't really attend to your exit or the separation. Without the treat, they're likely to stress out and whine right away, and once separation anxiety begins, it grows and grows in intensity over time. If they're otherwise engaged, however, the separation anxiety never starts in the first place. Since they didn't panic during the first minutes of your exit and absence, they'll be okay.

Separation anxiety is among the most common issues we treat at the Zoom Room. We see this problem far too often, and it's sad, because it's a miserable condition that is born out of misplaced passion and affection, or from a dog who was neglected in the past.

It's almost easier to explain the condition by giving you the perfect formula for how to *give* a dog separation anxiety. To make a dog truly miserable, create a huge tearful melodrama every time you leave home. Indulge in a lengthy goodbye replete with hugs and kisses. And then, every time you return home, dash to your dog and wrap them in your arms with thousands of kisses while telling them how much you missed them.

From a certain perspective, this could seem deeply loving. Unfortunately, this is just not how dogs operate. If you followed those instructions (please don't) your dog will be profoundly stressed out every time you leave or prepare to depart. They will suffer when you're gone.

If making your puppy suffer sounds like a terrible idea, simply do the opposite of the above recipe for disaster. Treat exits and returns as nonevents. We're not saying you shouldn't be madly in love with your puppy. Just wait until you've already been back home for a few minutes and *then* heap on the love. In a perfect world, your puppy grows up to be a dog who is only mildly excited when you come home. This may not sound ideal from your perspective, but it's an important sign of an emotionally stable dog.

Training Tips

Random crating: From time to time during the day, put your puppy in the crate for no reason at all, not because you're going out, not for potty training. Why? Random crating helps break the association that crate time is always paired with you leaving the house. It normalizes the crate and makes it more routine. This is an excellent practice for maintenance of good crate training. It's also a necessity during potty training whenever you're unable to provide dedicated supervision.

The crate is never a punishment: If you're feeling angry or frustrated with your puppy, never send your puppy to the crate punitively. "Go to your room" doesn't work with puppies and will significantly interfere with crate training.

Don't bang on the crate: Don't shake it, either. Your puppy will deeply dislike either of these and will come to view the crate as a form of punishment.

Using the crate during cleanup: Since accidents happen, there may come a time when your puppy has pooped in the house or chewed up a pillow and mess is everywhere; you want to get the place clean without a puppy underfoot. The crate is a natural solution. That said, you're probably not feeling thrilled about cleanup duty. Control your frustration. The crate must always be a place of thoughtful confinement, not a jail cell. Toss a treat in the crate as you invite them in, and praise them just as you would if there weren't a huge mess to tackle. You're miserable, but it must be happy time for your puppy whenever the crate is involved.

When you take a shower: Clients sometimes ask us what they should do when they have to take a shower. Easy. Bring the crate into the bathroom with you. Nearness is good. Or, if you know for sure that their bladder is empty (see Potty Training), you can leave them in their playpen while you bathe.

Don't be a homebody: While some new puppy owners struggle with balancing home, puppy life, and work life, enlisting the aid of friends, family, and dog walkers to ensure their puppy is well attended while they're away during the day, others can be home all day, but this presents a different issue. Being home all day long isn't an ideal training environment for your puppy. They need to get used to your leaving from time to time. If you're home *too* much, it can actually slow down crate training. So, force yourself to leave the house from time to time, if only to run a brief errand.

Transitioning Out of the Crate

Now that we've talked about where to locate the crate in your home, many people will be wondering how much longer that thing is going to sit there. It's a good question, and the answer is: it really depends...

Some people like to keep the crate as a permanent fixture, like an indoor doghouse. This is absolutely fine.

Many will want to ditch the crate as soon as possible, relegating it to storage. It's a good idea to keep your crate, as they're wonderfully useful for travel. See Traveling with a Crate for more details.

The two benchmarks: If eliminating the crate is your goal, it's safe to assume your puppy will be a year old before you remove the crate from your home, though you might be able to do so sooner. You're waiting for two benchmarks: 1) when they're fully potty trained (which will occur first), and 2) when they can be fully trusted to have the run of the house without causing damage (which comes later and varies greatly from puppy to puppy).

Don't rush it: Most people want to have a dog who can reliably stay at home without being crated. However, if the transition out of the crate is attempted too soon, your puppy may slide back into having more accidents and reverse your prior training. Only when your puppy is reliably crate trained and on a regular schedule can you give them more freedom. How will you know if they're ready?

Test the waters: Assuming you *believe* your puppy is now potty trained and crate trained, you're going to put these assumptions to the test. Without using a crate, confine your dog to your kitchen or some other single room and leave home for an hour. When you return, is your home in order and accident free? If so, repeat this test but stay away for three hours. Did they pass? Now expand your puppy's access to more of your home and leave for a 20-minute walk or a trip to the grocery store. Does everything look good when you return? Continue in this fashion by expanding your puppy's access until it encompasses the entire house, and by increasing the duration of your absence to ensure there is neither destruction nor accidents.

Don't rush it: Yes, this is a repeat. But it's so important we just had to say it twice. Remember: work slowly and don't expect too much too quickly. Better to thoughtfully confine your puppy than to undo all your hard work by giving them too much freedom too soon.

STEP 3

potty training

There's no getting around the subject. You have a puppy. You're going to be on cleanup duty. Potty training starts on day one, but it's going to take time. Time and lots and lots of paper towels.

This isn't going to be glamorous work, but if you have the right equipment and know-how, you're both going to do just fine.

It's important to recognize that whatever your puppy's breed or size, when they arrive home, they will not be able to make it through the night without peeing. If trained properly, all puppies will be able to sleep pee-free through the night by six months of age, and the vast majority will hit this milestone much sooner.

Puppy Perspective

When your puppy was with their mother and littermates, they would go to the bathroom wherever and whenever they desired. Their bladder muscle was not at all developed, so holding it in was impossible. The one instinct they were born with was an aversion to relieving themselves where they sleep.

On the day they arrive in their new home, that's still the state they're in: not yet able to hold it in. Over time, their bladder muscle will strengthen, giving them the physical ability to wait. Starting potty training on the day of their arrival will help considerably.

Bladder gauge: The rule of thumb is that your puppy can hold it in for roughly one hour per month of age. At two months, that means they can hold it for about two hours.

Creatures of habit: Puppies like to return to the same spot to go to the bathroom. This is going to be a major asset in potty training. Urine is like a fingerprint to dogs, with their keen sense of smell. Even young puppies are developing the ability to recognize the gender, age, and other identifying features of other dogs just by taking a whiff of their urine. So, when your puppy goes out for a walk, they're also in essence catching up on social media. And once they reach adolescence, they'll be tweeting and posting all over the neighborhood.

What "You" Means

As a reminder of what we wrote in the introduction to this book, if you're gone from the house all day, a puppy isn't the right choice for you unless you have a stand-in. A stand-in could be a member of your household who's home during the day, a neighbor or relative who will be lending a hand during the puppy's early months, or a dog walker. To keep things simple, in this chapter if we say "you" should take your puppy to potty, we mean you or your designated sitter.

Successfully Potty Training Your Pup

To successfully potty train your pup, consistency and patience are key.

Designate an area: Depending on where you live, your puppy's designated potty area might be a spot in your yard or a place close to your front door out on the sidewalk. Choosing to have an indoor potty area is only an option if you have a small breed and if you intend for your puppy to always relieve themselves inside your home when they're an adult, like a cat with a litter box. To create an indoor potty, simply lay a puppy pad on the floor in the spot where you want them to go and optionally add a chemical attractant if one is not already embedded in the material. Again, this is not a viable option for large breeds because the volume of urine output as your puppy grows will quickly become too much for a puppy pad.

Stick to one area: Remember, puppies like to return to the same place to go potty. This spot should be free of distractions. Designating a particular surface (gravel, for example) can help train your puppy to only go in the gravel, as puppies usually become conditioned to and prefer one surface over another. Alternatively, if your designated area is grass, your puppy will likely feel uncomfortable urinating on the concrete in a big city.

Indoor cleanup: For indoor potty areas, toss the soiled puppy pad, and clean with enzyme-based cleanser just in case there was some splatter. Some puppy owners like to leave the pee-soaked pads where they are, to encourage the puppy to return to the same spot. We're not fans of leaving messes on the floor, so we recommend cleaning up and using chemical attractant sprays on pads.

What about the weather?: You might be thinking that during the daytime, you'll take your puppy outside, but if it's the middle of the night and it is raining or freezing out, you'd prefer to have them just go on some puppy pads indoors. That is not a solid option. You're training your puppy where they will go to the bathroom when they're grown up. If you don't want them going inside, then keep a parka or raincoat near your bedside: rain, snow, sleet, or hail, you're taking them out to go potty. Welcome to puppy parenthood.

Take your puppy out frequently: You should provide breaks for your puppy after every meal, first thing in the morning, last thing at night, and several times in between during the day. Young puppies often have to urinate every 40 minutes. This means you have a "safe zone" of about 20 to 30 minutes before you have to start thinking about another break.

Time is of the essence: When it's time for a potty break, your puppy is really, really going to need to pee. Make a beeline. If you're using an indoor potty, simply pick up your puppy and place them on the puppy pad. If you live in a high-rise, and you have an elevator ride and some hallways to get through before you reach the great outdoors, your best bet is to pick your puppy up—they most likely won't pee in your arms—and carry them to the designated spot. Having them walk this gauntlet is likely to result in hallway and elevator accidents.

Using a leash: Unless you're using an indoor potty, you'll want to put your puppy on a leash. Even if you're carrying your puppy in your arms, bring the leash with you to attach as soon as you put them down. We'll cover leashes in much more detail in Leash Walking and Coming When Called. For now, simply understand that this isn't about loose leash walking. If it were, we'd have them in a harness, but there's no time to put your puppy in a harness every time they need to pee, and we don't leave the puppy wearing a harness all the time as it would chafe and your puppy would chew on the straps.

Leashes limit distractions: All you need to know about leashes during potty training is never to yank, tug, or pull on the leash. The leash is there to limit distractions. Once your puppy gets outside, they're greeted by a universe of fascinating stimuli. A puppy sometimes will get so distracted they'll forget they have to go to the bathroom. The leash restricts your puppy's roam to their designated potty area and keeps them focused on the matter at hand.

Hurry Up!: Give a *Hurry Up* command as they begin to eliminate. Eventually, your puppy will become conditioned to go when they hear this phrase, which comes in very handy when it's raining or freezing cold.

Reward good behavior: After they go, praise your puppy warmly and enthusiastically and reward with a treat. The focus is on positive motivation.

Get your puppy on a schedule: Feeding times should occur at the same time every day. Consistent feeding times usually result in consistent elimination times.

Be patient when you take your puppy outside: Sometimes, you will have to wait until nature calls. If, however, after 10 minutes your puppy still hasn't gone, take them back inside and immediately crate them. Wait 20 minutes and try again.

Wait for them to finish: Allow freedom only after your puppy is "empty." After your puppy has done their business, you may allow them some freedom to romp around inside your home, with supervision, of course.

Pee versus poop: You'll notice that this chapter is very pee-centric. Pee is very predictable and mathematical, relating directly to when they drink water. For young puppies, the frequency can be as high as every 40 minutes. As their bladder muscle strengthens and you get them on a schedule, they will be able to hold it for longer periods of time. Poop, on the other hand, varies considerably from puppy to puppy. Your puppy will poop on a regular schedule, but it will take you a couple of days or weeks to learn their schedule. Some puppies poop twice a day; some six times a day. Keep your feeding times and amounts consistent, and pay attention to your puppy's pooping habits. Some people even like to keep a journal or use a tracking app.

Poop Inspection

Your puppy's poop can serve as an indication of their health and how their diet is working. It's best to get in the habit of at least glancing at their poop before you toss it. Your puppy's poop should be firmly formed stool.

While there are regional variations, the most common form of parasite—really extremely common in puppies, no matter where your puppy came from—is tapeworms. This infestation happens when your puppy eats an infected flea. These worms will look like little white grains of rice in the poop. If you do see tapeworms, collect a small amount of infected feces in a container and store it in the refrigerator. Take your puppy to the vet. And don't forget to bring that container!

Diarrhea can mean something or nothing. It's not that different than with humans. If you had diarrhea, you might not make much of a fuss, but if it lasts a few days, you'll likely consult a doctor. Same thing with your puppy.

Scratching, itching, and biting their own skin are common signs of a food allergy or intolerance, but so is diarrhea. If the food you're now feeding your puppy is significantly different from what they had been eating before you brought them home, you can expect loose stool for a few days. If these signs of food allergy or intolerance continue beyond a few days, take your puppy to the vet. If diarrhea is one of the symptoms, you should collect and bring a stool sample.

Constipation is most often caused by dehydration—a sign that your dog is not drinking enough water. It can also be an indication that you're not taking them out to poop frequently enough. The longer that poop sits inside your puppy, the more moisture is absorbed into their body, leaving the poop dryer and harder.

Lastly: poopy butt. Especially for dogs with lots of fur or hair on their butts, when their poop is soft or loose, it can end up caked around their anus. Not only will this track poop into your house, but the close proximity of the poop to their skin can cause a rash or even an infection. If your dog has an especially furry butt, we recommend that either you or a groomer trim around the area to keep the hair very short for just this reason. If your puppy does have a poopy butt, help them avoid getting an infection or making a mess by promptly cleaning their posterior with either baby wipes or—if it's too dry and hard—a washcloth soaked in warm water.

Communication: If the "you" in your puppy's life will include other members of your household, a dog walker, or others, be sure that when you leave for work in the morning you let the responsible party know whether or not your dog has pooped, when they last peed, and other such fun stats.

Be a good neighbor: Responsible dog ownership takes many forms. One of the simplest is remembering to always pick up after your dog. While it's true that it won't make any difference to your puppy, it will make your neighborhood a nicer place and contribute to more positive attitudes toward dogs in your community. Never leave home without poop bags.

The Zoomies

We're often asked where the name "Zoom Room" came from. Our indoor dog training gym is a room where dogs can get out their "zoomies" in a positive way. Don't know what zoomies are? You're about to find out. They're a sure sign that your puppy is ready for bed.

Around 7 to 8 p.m., you will likely see your puppy explode with a huge burst of very naughty energy. They may zip back and forth across the living room at full speed. They may start nipping at your toes and generally acting feisty in ways you hadn't really seen before.

You might think this is a sign that they need more exercise. It isn't. This is the zoomies. Adult dogs get the zoomies for various reasons, but usually it's because they have excess energy to burn off. But for a puppy at 7 p.m., it is a sign they are utterly exhausted and ready to crash. Let them burn it off a bit, then put them in their crate.

The Schedule

Here's a helpful schedule of how to fit potty training into your day. Feel free to modify it to suit the demands of your own household.

Good morning: When you first wake up in the morning, even before you've had your coffee, take your puppy out of their crate and take them to their designated area to pee. Remember the instructions: *Hurry Up*, remain patient, wait for the finish, praise, and treat. Make a mental note as to whether they pooped or not until you learn their rhythm.

All business: Both your puppy and you have successfully completed all the steps. Now what? Now you pick your puppy up or walk them back inside. Remember they're still not fully vaccinated, so we're not going to explore the neighborhood today. This isn't outdoor playtime. We visited the potty, and now we go back and reset.

Breakfast in bed: Back to the crate for breakfast. If they haven't pooped yet, keep them in their crate for 20 to 30 minutes while you get ready for your day.

Post-jentacular poop: Post-jentacular is an awesome word for "after breakfast." Now you can return to the potty area. *Note: if your puppy pooped first thing in the morning, you can skip this excursion.* The majority of puppies will need to poop after they've eaten. Your puppy may need to pee again, too. Follow the same instructions as always. Hang out for about 10 minutes, keeping it all business without engaging in play or banter. If they haven't pooped after 10 minutes, head back inside and return them to their crate for another 20 to 30 minutes, then try again.

After they've pooped: Once your puppy has had their first poop of the day, you know that they are empty, and this means they can enjoy supervised playtime outside of their crate in a confined area using closed doors, puppy gates, or a playpen. Now is a wonderful time to pull out some chew toys or a tug toy for a game of tug.

Playtime leads to potty time: Romping around causes a puppy to need to pee and/or poop. After about 10 to 15 minutes of play, take your puppy out to potty again. Remember to go potty after every play session.

Now they're exhausted: By now your puppy is exhausted, if they haven't already collapsed into a nap. This is really your puppy's day: alternating periods of playing, pottying, and napping. If they haven't napped yet, put them in their crate by following the steps in **Crate Training**: show treat, say *Crate* as you toss in a treat, say *Yes* when they enter, close door, praise warmly. If they ever plop down into a nap outside of their crate, let them sleep as long as they're in a confined area and you can continue to keep an eye on them; when they wake up, they will need to pee straight away.

After nap: Just as you head to the designated potty area after every playtime, you do likewise right after every nap. At this point you should recognize that you are providing so many bathroom breaks and so much supervision that your puppy hasn't had a single opportunity to have an accident. This is successful potty training at its best. However, accidents can happen—that's why they're called accidents—so if they do, see the Troubleshooting section at the end of this chapter (**here**).

Lunch: While feeding your puppy twice a day is okay, we recommend that puppies eat three meals a day. And as you'll see in the next chapter (**here**), we do not recommend ever allowing free-feeding. Assuming you'll be feeding your puppy three times each day, you should expect a midafternoon poop.

Afternoon: This is a repeat of the earlier part of the day. Playtime. Potty. Naptime. Potty. Remember to never leave your puppy unattended. If your eyes can't be on them, keep them in their crate.

Evening: In many households, the time just before dinner often includes an increase in excitement; family members are getting home from work or school, so there may be some extra playtime now. This is all good as long as you remember that potty breaks always follow playtime.

Post-prandial poop: Post-prandial is an awesome word for "after dinner." After dinner, no great surprise, your puppy will need to poop and pee again.

Remove the water: The actual time will vary depending on your household, but roughly two hours before your own bedtime, you should take away your puppy's water. Puppies don't know when to stop drinking, and if they keep drinking throughout the night, you can kiss a good night's sleep goodbye.

Bedtime for puppy: Keep playtime brief before bedtime. If you put your puppy to bed at 9 p.m., then from 8 to 9 p.m. keep your interactions calm and mellow. This isn't a good time for tug-of-war games. If you have an older dog who loves to play with the puppy, this isn't a good time for that, either. A nice calm choice is to give your puppy a tendon to chew on. It's enjoyable but not all that stimulating. Then take your puppy out for one last potty break, and bring them back in. It's now about 9 p.m., and you place them in their crate to sleep.

Your own bedtime: Let's say your own bedtime is around 11 p.m. or midnight. You might want to wake your puppy up for a pee break just before you go to bed. This can often, but not always, obviate the need to wake up in the middle of the night for a 3 a.m. potty break. It's perfectly fine to wake your puppy up in this scenario. Important: *How* you wake your puppy makes a difference. If you reach into the crate to wake your puppy with your hands, the sleeping dog's instincts could kick in, perceiving a predator. Instead, use a calm, soothing voice to rouse your pup. Only once they're awake should you handle them.

In the middle of the night: Remember: initially your puppy's crate is ideally going to be located in your bedroom. So, you'll hear them when they whine. And you will hear whining, especially during the first few nights when they are lonely and missing their littermates. But they'll also whine because they have to go to the bathroom and are stressed out about peeing inside the crate where they sleep. Admittedly, at first it's very difficult to know the difference between lonely whining and potty whining. When you hear whining, wait. If the crate is next to your bed, you can put your hand down next to the crate, so your puppy knows they are not alone. But don't talk to them. If they calm down, stop whining, and go back to bed, they were just lonely. But if they don't calm down and continue to whine, or the whining increases, err on the side of caution. Assume they have to pee and take them out of the crate to their designated area. Keep it businesslike—no playful interactions. It should just take a couple of minutes, then they go back in their crate and you go back to bed. If it's taking more than a couple of minutes, your puppy just wanted your attention, so head back inside and put your puppy in their crate and you in your bed.

You might be wondering why in crate training we stress the importance of not letting your puppy out of the crate until they are quiet, but here we're advocating letting them out in the middle of the night when they are relentlessly whining. It's a good question, and the answer is that these are very different situations. During the day, they're whining simply to get out of the crate, and that's not a behavior you wish to reward. But at night, it is extremely likely that they have a very legitimate reason for vocalizing—they have to go to the bathroom really bad—which is why we advise erring on the side of caution.

Troubleshooting

What to do if you find an accident: If you find an accident, do not go back and scold your puppy. Remember that it isn't their fault for going to the bathroom; it's a sign that you didn't anticipate their need and provide proper supervision. It's so important to remember that if you scold your puppy, they will be unable to make any connection at all between your displeasure and their having gone to the bathroom. That ship sailed a long time ago. Accidents happen. So, in addition to never scolding your puppy, also go easy on yourself.

If you catch your puppy in the act: Startle them with a nonresponse marker: say *Ah ah* and clap your hands. If they were caught peeing, they will likely stop midstream. Immediately pick them up and take them to their usual potty spot. If they were caught pooping, they may not be capable of stopping, and you will have no choice but to let them finish. Do not yell at them, as this will only make things worse. Try not to lose your temper. We'll cover the nonresponse marker in greater detail in The Six Key Commands (here), but for now, understand that it translates to "Nope, that's not the behavior I was looking for." It does *not* translate to "Bad dog."

If they were caught in the act of peeing, when you get to the potty area your puppy will likely finish going. Shift your demeanor and praise them warmly. If they finished going inside the house, simply take them back inside without any anger or fuss. After two or three "caught" accidents, your puppy will likely understand that this is not a desirable behavior. Remember: "caught in the act" means exactly that, not 30 seconds after the fact.

Accident cleanup is critical: Clean up all accidents with an enzyme-based cleaner as recommended in Puppy Supplies Checklist (here). When accidents occur, it is usually the result of too much freedom for the puppy, too little supervision from the human, too infrequent potty breaks, or a combination.

Accidents inside the crate should *never* happen. Remember, your puppy has a deep desire to never go to the bathroom where they sleep. One possibility is that you purchased a crate that is too big for them. Remember, they should only have enough room to turn around and lie down comfortably and no more than that. You may need a smaller crate or to readjust the dividers. If crate size is not the issue, definitely reread this chapter. If you're providing potty breaks at all the right times, crate accidents should not occur.

If your puppy regularly does soil their own crate, this is a habit they picked up before you brought them home that interfered with their instincts. In such a case, you will need the help of a professional trainer to undo this damage.

Intentional accidents: We mean intentional by you, not your puppy. Even the best-laid plans sometimes go astray, so there may be a day when you absolutely must leave for a while and you were unable to find a dog walker or neighbor to stop by during your absence to take your puppy potty. If you find yourself in this situation, it isn't ideal, but it will be okay. Here's what you should do:

Understand that your puppy will have to go potty in your absence, so therefore do not crate them. Instead, erect their pen and leave them in that confined area with some safe toys and chews to enjoy, ones you've previously supervised them with and know to be okay. Set a puppy pad on the floor or a couple of pads if the puppy is larger.

When you return home, clean up the mess without any reprimand. We want your puppy to have only one potty area, not two. But this was a special exception and it will be fine. Do take extra care to clean up the area surrounding the pad with an enzyme-based cleaner, so your puppy will be less tempted to reuse this temporary potty spot.

Spiteful "accidents": We're including this section only because it's a question that comes up frequently. People ask us if their dog is pooping or peeing in the house to express anger or resentment, to intentionally communicate their displeasure. The answer is a resounding no, this is not what is happening. Dogs do not do this. But since people ask, here's the answer:

Research has shown that a dog's range of emotions is vaster than previously understood. That said, they do not understand the concept of "revenge." They don't know how to be spiteful. A classic mistake of dog owners is anthropomorphizing; it can be dangerous to do so. If you think your puppy is angry at you and that's why they soiled the rug, you miss out on the real cause, which is probably poor training, separation anxiety, or a medical issue.

A very specific complaint we have heard all too often is, "Whenever I leave the house my dog poops in my bed. It's revenge. They're getting back at me for leaving." But that's not the case.

The dog probably has separation anxiety. The place in your home with the most concentrated smells of you is your bed. You could wash your sheets every day, but your mattress and pillow still give off your scent. Scared, lonely dogs and puppies will gravitate toward this concentrated smell to feel a sense of comfort, and because separation anxiety commonly causes bowel control issues, the purely *accidental* pooping happens in your bed. It's still an accident. Not a communication. Not an expression of anger or displeasure.

STEP 4

preventing food aggression

Food-aggressive dogs react with growling, snapping, or biting when people or other animals come anywhere near something the dog is eating. Dogs with this trait can be extremely dangerous to others. While it's possible to eliminate this behavior in older dogs, there's no time like when they are a puppy to prevent this problem from ever developing. One of the most effective ways to prevent food aggression is to hand-feed your puppy a few meals in their first few weeks with you. What may seem like a frustrating waste of time is actually a solid training strategy that will pay dividends further down the line.

Puppy Perspective

Modern domesticated dogs have inherited from their wolf ancestors a deep-seated anxiety related to where and when they will have their next meal. A dog could be pampered in a swanky penthouse, but deep down they will still have this innate food insecurity. You want your puppy to develop a relationship with you that is built on trust; specifically, they need to trust that you are there only to give them food, and not to take their food away.

Prevention: Hand-Feeding

With a new puppy, we have a wonderful opportunity to teach them that yours is the hand that gives and doesn't take. This is accomplished by hand-feeding their entire meal to them, one piece of kibble at a time.

Dine together: Since you are likely still crate training, you'll do this while they're in their crate with the door open and you seated nearby. You should do it a few times during the first few weeks you have them. If you have other members of your household (anyone other than a too-young child) all of you should take turns doing this a few times each.

One kibble at a time: The process is simple. Your puppy is in their crate. Portion out their entire dinner into a bag that you hold in your hand. Feed them a single piece of kibble at a time, letting them take it from the palm of your hand. You can speak to them reassuringly while they dine. That's it.

Training: Drop It

The most important thing to know about preventing food aggression is teaching your puppy that your hand never takes food away. Even if they have something in their mouth they shouldn't (which your puppy will do; every puppy will at some time put something in their mouth that they shouldn't), you never ever try to pull it out of their mouth unless it's a true emergency.

If you try to yank food, toys, shoes, or anything out of their mouth, they're learning the opposite lesson: that you're not to be trusted, that yours is the hand that takes food away. This lack of trust can cause your puppy to run from you when they have an object in their mouth or even to be afraid of your hands. Worse, this may foster aggression in your puppy.

Instead of prying items out of their mouth, you will deal with these inevitable situations by using a barter system and the command *Drop It*.

Before this situation occurs organically, for training purposes let's artificially create a scenario to teach them to release what's in their mouth in favor of something better.

Step 1: Give your puppy something other than food to have in their mouth. A chew toy or a tug is perfect.

Step 2: Put a delicious treat in front of their nose and say *Drop It*. Don't use a stern or angry tone of voice. Be very matter-of-fact with no sense of urgency.

Step 3: When your puppy drops the toy, say *Yes*, and pick up the toy as you give them the treat.

As soon as you finish, repeat Steps 1 to 3 a few times. In other words, after they eat the treat, give them back their toy. Let them enjoy it for a few moments, and now you're back at Step 1. This also helps in trust building, since your puppy sees that although you sometimes take away the toy, you also are the one who gives it back.

Training tips

Your puppy wants to trade up: If they don't drop the toy in favor of the treat, that means either the toy was too high value or more likely the treat wasn't motivating enough, or perhaps you forgot that training should be done on an empty stomach. Make sure the treat you offer is more rewarding than the toy, and that your puppy is sufficiently hungry to go for the trade.

Yours is the hand that gives: With *Drop It*, your puppy learns that the only time you take something is when you're also giving something of great value. And that you never take anything directly from their mouth.

Repeat to build associations: Repeat this training a few times each day. Once your puppy has learned *Drop It* and has developed fond associations, you will be able to use the command the next time they actually pick up in their mouth something that they shouldn't.

Don't give chase: If—or rather, *when*—your puppy gets something in their mouth they shouldn't, always resist the temptation to chase them around the house to get it from them. Your puppy will always perceive chasing as a game. Puppies love to be chased.

Create a distraction instead of chasing: You're better off finding a good distraction, anything that is more interesting than the thing in their mouth. This could be a delicious treat or a squeaky toy. Sometimes simply sitting on the floor will convince a puppy to come to you instead of running away. Get their attention with the distraction in order to make them forget all about that game they were just trying to play.

Use *Drop It* **after creating a distraction:** If by now your puppy hasn't already dropped the thing in their mouth in favor of the new game or distraction, you'll be in a perfect position to use your *Drop It* command.

Puppies and Kids

You should always keep young children away from your puppy while your puppy is eating or chewing on a bone. Puppies and dogs tend to view all children as equals, more like other puppies than people. They will therefore have a natural mistrust and wariness around kids.

In normal playtime activities, you don't need to be concerned. But during feeding time, keeping kids away is a good idea to ensure safety for the children and to prevent any food-aggression bad habits in your puppy.

Growling

If your puppy growls at you when they have something in their mouth, this is a sign that they don't trust you and are concerned you are going to take away their "resource."

Don't dominate your puppy: The worst thing you could do in this situation is to believe the common misperceptions about so-called dominance and think, "I'll show them who's boss." Do not try to lord over your puppy and establish some kind of dominance. Puppies just don't think this way, and you could end up with a serious bite.

Establish trust: Most importantly, take this growling as a sign that you should work more on building up trust by spending more time training with your puppy. Work on *Drop It*, but also work on Name Game, *Come*, *Sit*, and all the other training commands we'll cover in Socializing Your Puppy and The Six Key Commands. If they are growling, do another hand-feeding of their whole meal while they're in their crate with the door open. Generally, spend more time with your puppy showing them why you're the benevolent, nonaggressive leader from whom all things wonderful and delicious emanate.

GROWLING SCENARIO TIPS

If your puppy is chewing on a toy or bone, and as you near them they

growl: Follow the instructions for *Drop It* using a very high-value treat, something incredibly special. But then, after giving them the treat, also return their toy or bone. In this way, your puppy will learn that you might sometimes take a coveted item away but that you will also give it back.

If your puppy is chewing on something inappropriate, like a shoe, and as you near them they growl: Follow the instructions for *Drop It*, but since you are going to permanently take away something very exciting, special, and novel, you need to be sure to reward heavily. Have some very high-value treats available, and when your dog drops the object, spend about 30 seconds praising them and giving them the special treats one at a time. If the item they are chewing on is dangerous or so special that you can't risk them chewing on it for even the minute it might take you to go get the treats, then do something sudden and spontaneous that will surprise your puppy and cause them to drop the item to investigate. For example, you could drop to the ground a few feet away and make silly noises. Your unexpected behavior and odd sounds will likely cause your puppy to come investigate. Remember, puppies are inherently curious. Use this to your advantage.

If your puppy is eating their dinner, and when you pass nearby they growl: Simply give them some distance. Don't do anything else. Wait for them to be hungry again, even if it's the next day, and go back to the instructions for spending more time training and playing with your puppy. Develop trust in order to remind them that you are the most resplendently awesome creature in the world who provides all things desirable and that you can be trusted not to steal their food.

It's important to have a regular schedule and not to free-feed your puppy. Here are the reasons why.

Health: Pet obesity is a serious issue in the United States and has reached epidemic proportions. It's important to adhere to the recommendations of your vet or the bag of dog food for the correct amount to feed your puppy based on their age and weight.

If your puppy eats their food and still seems hungry, perhaps pawing at his bowl or whining, you must ignore this. You know you gave them the correct amount. Your puppy is not the authority on what their own body needs. Why? Dogs by their very nature will always worry about when their next meal will come, so if presented with an opportunity to eat, they will eat or, more to the point, overeat.

Training: Hunger is always your ally when you train. If your puppy is never hungry, training will be extremely difficult or even impossible.

Diagnosis: Appetite is an important indicator of your puppy's health. By keeping your puppy on a regular feeding schedule, you will promptly notice any significant changes, and this is something your vet will want to know.

Potty training: A regular feeding schedule leads to a regular pooping schedule, which makes potty training more of a breeze. If your dog eats anytime, they will poop any old time.

Pest control: Leaving food out all day invites ants and other critters to infest their bowl and your home.

STEP 5

socializing your puppy

There is nothing more important for the future happiness and emotional stability of your puppy than early socialization, and plenty of it. Being exposed to a wide range of people, places, sights, smells, and other dogs in a safe, upbeat, and rewarding manner is how your puppy learns the key lesson that the world is a wonderful and amazing place to live.

While learning about and experiencing the world we live in is of course a lifelong journey for all of us, puppies have a short developmental window in which their experiences will deeply inform their future selves.

That window begins with birth and lasts until they are about 16 weeks old. Puppies will continue to play and explore after 16 weeks, but we're going to focus on this critical window of eight to 16 weeks of age when the simple choices you make each day will have a truly lasting impact on their well-being and happiness.

Puppy Perspective

There are lots of ways to learn about the world, but for puppies their pick will always be playtime. Puppies are driven by innate curiosity, a desire to sniff all new and strange things, and to meet and explore new people and animals. They test boundaries through playful expressions of their curiosity. They learn concepts of home, safety, friendly, rewarding, scary, yucky, and dull by engaging their natural curiosity with all they encounter.

Whether these interactions are positive or negative, they learn from them. The trick is to make great choices for your puppy and select the best opportunities for them to come away from this eight-week period with the realization that life is good and full of positive experiences.

But there's a real challenge here. The period from eight to 16 weeks of age happens to *also* be the first fear phase in your puppy's life. They may experience fear, perhaps at meeting strangers with facial hair. Although it's scary today, it might not be scary in a couple of days or weeks as long as you don't push it. A bad experience can truly last a lifetime. This is called *imprinting*.

Don't worry if your puppy exhibits irrational fear; it's likely temporary. Be sensitive, encouraging, and understanding, and more than likely they'll move past it, and the source of the fear won't be imprinted.

At this age, all puppies play more or less similarly, sniffing things out, rolling around submissively, deeply bowing in a play bow to get the fun started. These early gestures will take shape over time into the adult dog your puppy will one day become.

Socialization means celebrating your puppy's innate curiosity and unleashing their desire to explore the world through play. Your job is that of the "cruise director." You're going to curate your puppy's experience of the world by providing lots of well-chosen opportunities for them to be exposed to new things.

The interactions you'll select for your puppy include people, dogs and other animals, and environments.

Socializing with People

When exposing your puppy to people, begin with your inner circle of family and close friends, then widen your circle to include coworkers, neighbors, and strangers. Ultimately your goal is to expose your puppy to all kinds of people.

Remember: everything is new to your puppy. You have to see the world with the freshest of eyes. A man wearing shorts? This is new! People in uniform. In wheelchairs. With lots of facial hair. With high voices and deep bellowing voices. You want your puppy to meet them all.

The best and easiest way to ensure a positive interaction with a person is treats. Delicious treats should always be at the ready. Absolutely you should also include verbal praise and petting, but a tasty treat is the most surefire way to mark an interaction as a happy one.

You should give treats to others—again, this means starting with your household and friends—but eventually don't be shy about handing a treat to neighbors or strangers and asking them to give it to your pup.

One key is to keep it simple. Puppies don't need structured games. There's no need to create an activity like fetching a stick or chasing a ball. Of course, if your puppy loves these activities, by all means toss away. But your puppy will naturally play with people and settle into enjoying their company and closeness.

Not everyone knows how to greet a dog. Many will reach a hand right down over the puppy's head or snout to pat them there. It's better for people to lower themselves and let the puppy make the approach.

Besides arranging these encounters and providing treats, you have one job that's just as important: keeping an eye on your puppy's arousal level. What if you introduce your puppy to a man with a beard and a deep voice, and your puppy acts fearful, skitters away, hides between your legs for security, or scampers to the other side of the room?

The worst thing you could do at this point is force the interaction. You certainly don't want to punish your puppy, and forcing them to take part in something that today is scary, however irrational that may be, will be experienced by your pup as punishment.

The word "today" is the key. Your job is to witness their shy or anxious behavior and recognize right away that today wasn't the day for that experience. Simply leave. Go back to a familiar place with them. You must be your puppy's advocate; no one else will.

Say something polite like, "They're in a fear phase right now. Let's try this again another day," or "We're just learning to go out in public and this may have been a little overwhelming," and bid farewell.

But don't feel guilty; don't feel as though you did something unpleasant to your puppy. Don't give them treats as you exit to somehow "make up" for the negative interaction. All that will do is reward the fearful behavior. Whenever we reward any behavior, we solidify it. And this isn't something to reinforce.

And here we reach the most important takeaway about socializing a puppy: They must always experience the world on their own terms, not ours. Today wasn't the day for the bearded man. So, try again tomorrow. Tomorrow's another day.

Socializing with Dogs

Most of this section will be about playdates for your pup with other puppies and dogs, but we didn't want to leave out all the other creatures. You may well have a cat or other critter, and puppies can and will enjoy playtime with everything from hamsters to hens. If you do, see Socializing with Other Animals.

Playing with other dogs is so important for your puppy's development; they will build confidence, establish their own play style, and become an environmentally stable adult who isn't reactive around other dogs. That's the goal here. Remember Tenet #5 (here): what everyone really wants is a happy, calm, bombproof dog you can take out in public, and you get this by loads of early socialization.

Your job is to orchestrate these playdates so that you set your puppy up for success. This means finding the right setting, carefully selecting their playmates, keeping interactions brief, and always ending on a high note.

Start with the right place: Any contained area is perfect. This could be a room in someone's home or an enclosed yard. No need for the pups to have free rein of the place; keep the activity to a small living room–sized area.

Next, pick the perfect playdate: Absolutely any same-age puppy is just fine. They don't have adult play styles yet, so there's no need to be choosy. When it comes to adult dogs, you want to specifically opt for those who are calm by nature with a gentle style of play.

To know the play style of the other dog means you need to *know* this other dog; it's not a stranger on the street. This is important for another reason: health and safety. Right now, your puppy is under 16 weeks, which means they haven't yet had all of their vaccinations. So, any adult dog playmate you choose for your puppy must belong to someone you know and trust, and you must be able to confirm that the dog isn't sick and has had all their shots. If you don't personally know any suitable playmates, see Puppy Play Spaces.

Go off leash: You want the playmates to be off leash. You've already selected a safe, contained area so you won't have to worry about anyone running off. Why off leash? When your puppy is off leash, they can meet and greet the other dog using appropriate dog language and without getting entangled. A leash interferes with your puppy's natural greeting style and restricts their movement, which can cause fear reactions and nervousness. When dogs are on leashes, the humans tend to lean in over the pups, constantly untangling the leads and making them feel trapped. That looming presence above doesn't make for a positive playtime.

Dogs on leashes are led into the unnatural position of greeting one another face-to-face. Such interactions aren't preferred by dogs, and in a natural setting they'll limit that face time on their own. They want to get back around to the business end of the other dog and start sniffing.

Appropriate dog language: Now that the pups are off leash in a safe space, they can commence with playtime and butt sniffing.

Appropriate play gestures include bouncy play, floppy tail wagging, deep play bows, and—especially when one dog is older—submissive behaviors. A typical submissive behavior would be your puppy crawling over to the older dog, then rolling on their back to expose their belly.

Keep it simple: There's no need for any special prompts to get them to play. They'll take care of all the play behaviors on their own. You don't have to plan any kind of special activity or game. In fact, if you brought a ball or toy with you, that could really interfere by introducing negative behaviors like resource guarding as one or both of the dogs tries to hog the ball and keep the other away. Don't overthink it.

No treats needed: A question we're often asked is if these positive interactions should be rewarded with treats, to teach the puppy that playing with other dogs is a good thing. This is one of those rare instances where you yourself don't need to provide any positive reinforcement at all. Why? Because the joy of being with other dogs is itself the reward. This playdate you arranged was already the perfect present for your pup.

Keep it short and end on a high note: During playtime, your job is to stand back. Don't helicopter. But at the same time, you will be mindful of the time and the importance of ending on a high note. Keep the interaction brief—10 to 20 minutes is plenty of time, or shorter if your puppy seems tired or possibly losing interest.

Don't worry about being a killjoy: Go ahead and put your puppy back on their leash or into their carrier and lead them away at the peak of the merriment. Your puppy won't mind, for they will have nothing but the most positive associations of playing with other dogs and will be even more excited for the next playdate.

Troubleshooting puppy playdates: What if the playdate isn't going well? Your puppy might be shy or submissive around other dogs or puppies during their first playdates. You might feel worried that something is wrong with your puppy. Don't be. This is totally normal. Experiencing anxiety around other puppies or dogs is well within what is normal for a young puppy. What you want to do is make sure that they are safe (i.e., not engaged in play with a dog who plays too rough), and that they have somewhere to escape to, and that the other dogs are respecting that.

Your puppy should have somewhere—behind or under a chair, for example—where they can hang out and be by themselves. Make sure that wherever this place is, your puppy has a direct line of sight to see what the other dogs are doing.

Now just wait. Your puppy will eventually want to come out and get in on the action. Just remember not to force the interaction. Your puppy has to decide on their own that they want to come out and see what all the fun is about.

But what if your puppy isn't shy and retreating but rather starts to snap or growl at the other dogs during play? This is perfectly okay. Growling and snapping, in dog language, is a perfectly fine and acceptable form of communication that simply lets the other dogs know to give a little more personal space. So many humans see their pup growling and snapping and feel embarrassed or frightened, thinking it's rude or menacing, and feel worried that others may think you have a mean, aggressive dog. You don't; all you need to know is that the ones who really matter—the other dogs—totally understand this behavior and are fine with it. If your puppy growls or snaps at other dogs, don't punish this behavior: it is normal.

Socializing with Other Animals

As we mentioned earlier, you may have other critters in your house such as cats, birds, hamsters, and chickens. You can socialize your puppy with all of them, but extra care must be taken.

All puppies have some degree of prey drive, ranging from very mild to extremely acute. Never leave your puppy alone with another animal. Always keep your puppy on leash and maintain a safe distance. Over time, with careful monitoring and rewards, you can close the distance.

The most common household non-dog pet would of course be a cat. A great tip with cats is to first introduce your puppy to your cat through a closed door, allowing the new roommates to sniff each other under the door. You can use this same technique with other animals, too.

After they've "met" via door-sniff, you can progress to "in person" meetings with your puppy on leash at a safe distance. Go slow. Take your time. As with all things puppy, don't rush it.

A Trip to the Hardware Store

One of our favorite tips for our clients is to take young puppies to the hardware store for an outing. Luckily, almost every major hardware chain in America has a dog-friendly policy. The hardware store may seem to you like just a place to run an errand, but to your puppy it is a whole new universe of sights, sounds, and smells.

- Don't let your puppy walk around the store. Since these stores are dog friendly, adult dogs will have been there recently, and you want to keep your puppy safe.

- Bring a dog bed or blanket with you and place it in a shopping cart. Put your puppy in the cart. Wheel them gently and slowly up and down the aisles.

- Bring treats. *What you want to reward is anything other than fear or anxiety.* Try to view the store from your puppy's point of view. If a loud announcement comes over the speaker system, realize this could be frightening. If your puppy has no reaction at all, give them a treat. Announcements are good. Not freaking out at announcements is even better.

- Head over to the gardening section where there will be all kinds of different smells, all kinds of plants, fertilizers. Their nose is light-years better than ours. You don't have to hold up a bag of fertilizer to their nose. Just wheel past things. And keep giving treats throughout your adventure.

- Chat in a happy, playful voice with your puppy as you navigate the store. Reach down and pet them behind the ears from time to time. Outings are fun.
- The hardware store is full of all kinds of people who will be attracted to your adorable puppy. Encourage these visits and be liberal with the dog treats.
- As with all types of socialization, if your dog seems restless or anxious, whimpers or cowers or shakes, it's too much, and today isn't the day. Head home.
- Remember not to reinforce this fearful behavior; don't give treats to make your puppy feel better.
- If they're having a great time, remember to end on a high note. Give them a belly rub and some treats and head back home.

Socializing in Different Environments

While it's so important to expose your puppy to new places and experiences, safety is paramount. Until they're 16 weeks old, they haven't yet had all of their vaccinations, so a lot of the world is off limits.

Prior to 16 weeks, your puppy shouldn't go to any kennel or day care facility, nor to any dog park, no matter how tempting that may be. You don't want to worry about the risk of infection from adult dogs who may be ill and whose health and vaccination status you just don't know. Exceptions would be facilities with dedicated and sanitized puppy play spaces such as those mentioned here.

When you go to the vet, remember lots of adult dogs—and unwell ones at that—visit there, and while the staff will certainly keep the place clean throughout the day, you should avoid setting your puppy down on the floor or allowing them to interact with other animals. Keep them off the floor and in your lap, a carrier, or their crate.

When you go for walks, favor any kind of hardscape, sidewalks for example, over grassy areas. Germs that can cause infections will thrive far better on moist grass and planted areas than on flat, smooth, dry, and hard surfaces.

When you're out in the world with your puppy before they're 16 weeks, you need to keep a watchful eye: no drinking from another dog's water bowl, no sniffing at another dog's poop, and no interactions with unknown dogs.

All of this may make it seem almost impossible to get your puppy out into the great wide world, but it can be done. See A Trip to the Hardware Store for one great idea for puppies less than 16 weeks old.

Puppy Play Spaces

Depending on where you live, you might have access to a place that advertises playgroups or puppy socialization classes for young puppies.

While playdates with one or more puppies or dogs at your own place or a friend's home are absolutely fine, if you do happen to live somewhere where you can take advantage of organized puppy playgroups, those do provide a wonderful opportunity for your puppy to socialize with several same-age puppies at once. Such sessions also sometimes include helpful training tips.

But you do need to be highly selective and ask the right questions before attending such a playgroup. The majority of doggy day care facilities, for example, do not have a segregated area that is only for puppies, where no adult dogs are allowed to set foot. But some might, as well as some veterinary offices and *indoor* training facilities like the Zoom Room.*

Playgroups for eight- to 16-week-old puppies should not include puppies who are fully vaccinated (16- to 32-week-old pups). Those over 16 weeks are likely visiting dog parks, dog-friendly restaurants, and day cares and could therefore bring germs into the facility.

Also, puppies develop their adult play style right around 16 weeks of age. Mixing the two age groups is a dangerous mismatch. Eight- to 16-week-old puppies tend to play very gently; 16 weeks and older tend to play rough and really get into it. This can be way too much energy and roughhousing for a very young puppy.

* Because of these two reasons (vaccination levels and play styles) the Zoom Room offers two kinds of socialization options: Puppy Preschool for puppies eight to 16 weeks, which includes puppy training classes as well as playtime, and Puppy Playgroups for puppies 16 to 32 weeks, for older puppies who have had all their shots and have more

established play styles.

Here are the questions you should ask and get answered in writing before you take your puppy to a play space:

- **Is the play area fully indoors?** The answer needs to be yes, as it's the only way to ensure a fully sanitized area.

- **Is use of the play area limited only to puppies, and if not, is the area fully sanitized with veterinary-grade disinfectant prior to each and every puppy playgroup session?** The answer should be yes, only puppies, or yes, always sanitized.

- **Are all the participants puppies? What is the age range allowed?** The answer should be eight to 16 weeks or 16 to 32 weeks.

- **What is the maximum number of puppies?** This can vary, but 10 is a good maximum. Any number much larger is too difficult to manage well.

- **Are the playgroup sessions supervised by a trained and experienced dog trainer or behaviorist, as opposed to some other staff member?** The answer should be yes.

ADDITIONAL SOCIALIZING TIPS

Here are some additional tips for exposing your eight- to 16-week-old puppy to different environments:

- Hang out in front of a busy grocery store and ask admiring passersby to say hello to your puppy while you supply them with a stream of treats.

- Some department stores are dog friendly but rarely visited by dogs and kept so clean that it's okay to allow your puppy to walk about.

- Children's playgrounds and tot lots are a great place for your puppy to meet admiring children and grownups; just be mindful of any adult dogs.

- The lobby of a dog-friendly hotel is a wonderful place to take a seat and get comfortable with your puppy on your lap. Enjoy the ambience while folks come over and pet your pup.

- In general, look after your puppy's safety by using carriers or a crate, and avoid places frequented by adult dogs.

- For more ideas for dog-friendly places near you, see Resources.

Once your puppy is fully vaccinated, the world truly does become their oyster. Now you can and should take them everywhere. Just make sure you let your puppy experience the world on their own terms. Remember never to force it. If you decide you'd like to take them for a trip to the beach, a campground, a neighborhood block party, or to visit your coworkers at your place of employment, make sure your plans allow you to throw in the towel and go back home if needed.

Like socializing with other dogs, these interactions should be brief, upbeat, and end on a high note. The smells and sounds and sights of the ocean or lake or office are going to be brand-new for your puppy, and you have no way of knowing how they might react.

If they seem fearful, don't force it. Head home or somewhere else and try again another day. Neither punish nor reward them for not being up to this adventure today. Just move on.

But, on the other hand, if they're having a fantastic time, celebrate the moment with a handful of delicious treats. You're helping build positive associations with all the experiences that make up your world and that you're eager to share with them.

Puppy Socialization Checklist

It is important to create many positive experiences for your puppy during the critical socialization window which begins at birth and closes by 16 weeks. Pair your dog's favorite treat with the listed exposures. The goal is for your puppy to have fun and positive interactions. Remember, don't force your puppy to confront something when they're not ready. Allow them to go at their own pace and retreat when needed to feel safe. Use the checkboxes to track your dog's exposure to these different experiences. Third time's the charm! Have fun!

People

- ❏ ❏ ❏ Children standing and playing
- ❏ ❏ ❏ Toddlers walking and squealing
- ❏ ❏ ❏ Infants crawling
- ❏ ❏ ❏ Young adults
- ❏ ❏ ❏ Middle-age adults
- ❏ ❏ ❏ Senior citizens
- ❏ ❏ ❏ People with canes or walkers
- ❏ ❏ ❏ Loud, confident people
- ❏ ❏ ❏ Shy, timid people
- ❏ ❏ ❏ People wearing hats or helmets
- ❏ ❏ ❏ People wearing sunglasses
- ❏ ❏ ❏ Men with beards or facial hair
- ❏ ❏ ❏ Mail or delivery carriers
- ❏ ❏ ❏ People with backpacks or purses
- ❏ ❏ ❏ People wearing hoodies
- ❏ ❏ ❏ People carrying boxes
- ❏ ❏ ❏ People running by
- ❏ ❏ ❏ Indigent or homeless people
- ❏ ❏ ❏ People of different ethnicities

Objects

- ❏ ❏ ❏ Bicycles
- ❏ ❏ ❏ Skateboards
- ❏ ❏ ❏ Baby strollers
- ❏ ❏ ❏ Buses
- ❏ ❏ ❏ Shopping carts
- ❏ ❏ ❏ Garbage cans outside
- ❏ ❏ ❏ Wheelchairs
- ❏ ❏ ❏ Motorcycles
- ❏ ❏ ❏ Pots and pans
- ❏ ❏ ❏ Blankets or rugs being shaken
- ❏ ❏ ❏ Brooms
- ❏ ❏ ❏ Umbrellas
- ❏ ❏ ❏ Bags blowing in the wind
- ❏ ❏ ❏ Sidewalk signs

❏ ❏ ❏ Fire hydrants
❏ ❏ ❏ Large plastic garbage bags
❏ ❏ ❏ Hair dryers

Surfaces

❏ ❏ ❏ Concrete
❏ ❏ ❏ Slippery floors like hardwood or tile
❏ ❏ ❏ Stairs
❏ ❏ ❏ Grass
❏ ❏ ❏ Carpet
❏ ❏ ❏ Metal surfaces like exam tables
❏ ❏ ❏ Vet hospital scales
❏ ❏ ❏ Sand
❏ ❏ ❏ Gravel, stone, or pebbles
❏ ❏ ❏ Ice, frost, or snow

Animals

❏ ❏ ❏ Puppies who play well
❏ ❏ ❏ Friendly adult male dogs
❏ ❏ ❏ Friendly adult female dogs
❏ ❏ ❏ Cats
❏ ❏ ❏ Rabbits or small pets
❏ ❏ ❏ Horses
❏ ❏ ❏ Goats or sheep
❏ ❏ ❏ Fish in tanks
❏ ❏ ❏ Chickens

Sounds

❏ ❏ ❏ Fireworks
❏ ❏ ❏ Sirens
❏ ❏ ❏ Babies and kids
❏ ❏ ❏ Car horns
❏ ❏ ❏ Alarms
❏ ❏ ❏ Dogs barking
❏ ❏ ❏ Doorbells
❏ ❏ ❏ Vacuum cleaners

- ❏ ❏ ❏ Thunder
- ❏ ❏ ❏ Knocking on doors
- ❏ ❏ ❏ Trains
- ❏ ❏ ❏ Trucks
- ❏ ❏ ❏ Motorbikes

Handling

- ❏ ❏ ❏ Holding or cradling puppy
- ❏ ❏ ❏ Checking and cleaning ears
- ❏ ❏ ❏ Examining mouth and gums
- ❏ ❏ ❏ Touching all four paws
- ❏ ❏ ❏ Clipping toenails
- ❏ ❏ ❏ Touching tail
- ❏ ❏ ❏ Touching muzzle
- ❏ ❏ ❏ Hugging puppy
- ❏ ❏ ❏ Grabbing collar
- ❏ ❏ ❏ Touching rear legs
- ❏ ❏ ❏ Grooming with soft brush
- ❏ ❏ ❏ Putting on a harness
- ❏ ❏ ❏ Wiping body with a towel

Play

- ❏ ❏ ❏ Balls
- ❏ ❏ ❏ Tug toys
- ❏ ❏ ❏ Squeaky toys
- ❏ ❏ ❏ Puzzle toys or treat balls
- ❏ ❏ ❏ Cardboard boxes
- ❏ ❏ ❏ Buckets
- ❏ ❏ ❏ Stuffed toys
- ❏ ❏ ❏ Empty plastic bottles

Environment

- ❏ ❏ ❏ Dog-friendly events
- ❏ ❏ ❏ Dog training classes
- ❏ ❏ ❏ Car rides
- ❏ ❏ ❏ Suburban neighborhoods

- ❏ ❏ ❏ Residential city streets
- ❏ ❏ ❏ High-traffic city streets
- ❏ ❏ ❏ Parking lots
- ❏ ❏ ❏ Inside buildings
- ❏ ❏ ❏ Countryside
- ❏ ❏ ❏ Parks
- ❏ ❏ ❏ Pet stores

STEP 6

the six key commands

We've already covered crate training, potty training, and socializing. In this step we'll dive into the six commands every puppy should know. But why? Why train a puppy? There are three main reasons: mental stimulation, manners, and safety.

Puppies have brains, and they love to use them; they crave having a job to do. You also want your puppy to recognize you as the benevolent leader you are, and to follow your every command.

You train your puppy so that they'll be polite and well-mannered both at home and out in the world. You want to take them out in public with you, and these adventures should involve behaving wonderfully and obediently.

Starting training at a young age is also important for your puppy's safety, so they learn not to bolt out the door into the street or to leap from the car. And while all puppies start out small—their wagging tails and jumping paws can only do so much damage—some puppies will grow into enormous dogs. The way to prevent a huge dog from being unruly and accidentally hurting someone or knocking things over is to train them when they are still a little pup.

Puppy Perspective

Puppies are natural followers and are delighted to have a benevolent leader like you. They are also creatures of habit who thrive on patterns. This is good to know, for you're going to want these patterns to be on your terms, the schedule and habits that suit your household.

In terms of drive, all puppies want to chew on everything and jump on everyone. But they don't distinguish between positive and negative attention, praise versus scolding. That's why we don't teach puppies with punishment and no's. We're going to stick to positive rewards. The only attention they'll know is approval, and it will come when they obey as you teach your puppy that nothing in life is free. They might come with their own rambunctious drive, but you're going to teach them to, in effect, say please and thank you. You'll teach them to deeply *want* to act polite in exciting situations, because they will have learned through basic training that they will get love, approval, attention, and treats when they behave. The cost of these goodies is good manners. And the joy they'll get from your approval will greatly outweigh the chewing and jumping drive they were born with.

Reward Training Fundamentals

While you already know a few commands, this section will deepen your understanding of training.

THREE PHASES OF REWARD TRAINING

Positive reinforcement training means rewarding your puppy when they do what you want them to do. No matter what you're teaching your puppy, reward training will always move through three separate phases.

Phase 1: Luring and Baiting

You'll use the treat like a wand to direct the puppy toward what they should be doing. You move the treat through space to show what you want them to do.

> → Example: Showing the treat, then tossing it into the crate where you want your puppy to go.

Phase 2: Reward Every Time

Once your puppy has grasped the concept of what you were teaching in Phase 1, you move on to this phase, in which you no longer have to demonstrate what needs to be done. You just give the command and corresponding hand signal. And every single time they get it right, they get rewarded with a treat.

> → Example: Giving your puppy a treat every time they go into their crate when you say *Crate*.

Phase 3: Variable Reward

Once your puppy can do the behavior every time you give the command, you can start phasing out the treats. But don't just go cold turkey. The most powerful way of learning is through variable reward. That means, fairly randomly, that from here on out, sometimes when your puppy does the behavior, they get a treat; sometimes, they get verbal praise ("good dog!"), sometimes a pat on the head, sometimes nothing, sometimes a big handful of treats. You'll continue this phase throughout your dog's adulthood.

> → Example: Once your puppy knows *Crate* perfectly, sometimes reward them with "good dog!" and other times, randomly, give them one or a handful of treats when they enter their crate on command.

You'll move pretty quickly from one phase to the next. And as a handy little reminder of the three phases, you can remember LAB RETrieVeR. (**L**uring **A**nd **B**aiting. **R**eward **E**very **T**ime. **V**ariable **R**eward.)

TREATS VERSUS FUNCTIONAL REWARDS

A wonderfully fun part of having a puppy is learning what it is your puppy finds rewarding. A *functional reward* is one that is not food based. There are lots of functional rewards such as retrieving, tugging, physical affection, car rides, walks, chase games, and verbal praise in a high, excited voice. Not all puppies find all of those rewarding, but you'll soon know what your puppy loves.

You can and should use these functional rewards throughout the day, every day, to show your puppy that you like what they just did.

But when learning brand-new behaviors, which is what this chapter is all about, we're going to stick with treats.

As you go out together into the world, and your puppy's personality develops, you can extend rewarding to include functional rewards.

NOT ALL TREATS ARE CREATED EQUAL

In order to successfully train your puppy, treats should be just that: a treat. Be sure to select appropriate treats based on these criteria and utilize them often.

Avoid carb-based treats: Crackers, biscuits, and cookies take too long to chew, make a mess, leave distracting crumbs, tend to be empty calories, and are much less motivational. Remember: your puppy is technically an omnivore but profoundly at the *carnivore* end of the omnivore spectrum.

Stick to very small, soft, meat-based treats or cheese: Avoid using kibble; your puppy gets it all the time, so it isn't as rewarding, and it's also too crumbly and slow to chew. If you must use kibble to train, mix it in with highly rewarding treats.

Every moment of every day can be an opportunity for your puppy to learn: Since they'll be learning through treats, it's important to have plenty around all the time. The easiest way to do this is to purchase a treat pouch or bait bag which you can wear on your hip or belt. (See Puppy Supplies Checklist, here, for training gear recommendations.) A sealable plastic bag full of treats in your pocket or purse is fine, too, if it is always at the ready.

VERBAL MARKER: YES

One of the single most important differences between puppies and people is that puppies have a *tiny* window during which their brains can make an association between a behavior they just did and a reward that follows. *This window is only 1.3 to 1.5 seconds.*

Timing is everything: What does this mean? Let's say your dog sits on command. And you reach for a bag of treats, fish around in it, pull one out, then hand it to your dog seven seconds after they sat. You are too late. In fact, you're *much* too late. Too late for what? For them to learn that the reason you just gave them a treat is because they sat on command. They have no idea why you're giving them this gift and will associate it with whatever they happen to be doing at that exact moment. Which may be fine if they are still sitting calmly, but if they already moved out of the sit and are now standing, you have effectively rewarded them for standing.

Use a bridge: Because we are humans and not robots, it just might take us seven seconds to deliver the treat to our puppy. That's okay. Thankfully, there's a bridge called a Verbal Marker. Maybe you can't produce a treat in 1.3 seconds, but you can definitely say Yes in that short a time. And that's exactly what we do. So, in the previous example, as soon as your dog sits on command, you happily and immediately exclaim Yes and then you can fumble for that treat as quickly as you're able.

Now you might be asking yourself, the puppy clearly knows the treat is a reward because it tastes delicious, but how on earth do they know that Yes means they did the right thing? Dogs don't speak English. So how would they know?

That is an excellent question. And the answer is: they don't; they have no idea what it means. Until we teach them that Yes = treat. And that's the very first thing you'll teach them, by doing what we call "loading the verbal marker."

Loading the verbal marker: First you need to pick a verbal marker. We use *Yes* because it's quick and specific.

Learning by association: Now we're going to take a page from Pavlov, the scientist who did the pioneering work in learning by association by discovering that dogs salivated when they heard the sound of a bell after consistently pairing the bell sound with the appearance of food. We are going to teach your dog to associate *Yes* with treats.

Yes/Treat/Repeat: Sit down on the floor with your puppy and have a bag full of delicious soft meat treats, or an entire meal of kibble, at the ready. Say *Yes* in a happy tone and immediately give them a treat. Once they've swallowed the treat, do it again. *Yes*, treat. *Yes*, treat. *Yes*, treat.

In this critical activity, you're not teaching any kind of behavior. You're teaching the fundamental of the verbal marker, that *Yes* = treat. Having done this, you can proceed with the rest of the chapter and train your puppy who has now learned their first word: *Yes*.

NONRESPONSE MARKER: AH AH

A *nonresponse marker* is a communication to your dog that indicates they didn't execute the desired action. In addition to *Yes*, your dog will need to learn something that is along the lines of no, but not quite. "No" is a bit too strong. We want something that in the context of training means, "You're not in trouble, you didn't do anything bad, but that wasn't the behavior I was looking for."

We recommend using *Ah ah*. It's basically the same as "Uh uh" but has a higher, sharper pitch. A gentle "Nope" works well, too. In this book, we'll stick to *Ah ah*.

This nonresponse marker isn't something that you load the way you did *Yes*. Your puppy will learn it over time, as you train together, as long as you use *Ah ah* consistently.

Keep calm: Don't say *Ah ah* in anger or with any frustration in your voice. It's a simple cue to your puppy that the behavior they performed was not quite right.

For training sessions only: Don't use *Ah ah* outside of training sessions, for example if your dog is engaged in some kind of unwanted destructive behavior like chewing your shoes. Reserve this nonresponse marker only for training sessions.

PROOFING

Proofing is the process of training a dog to perform a behavior consistently, regardless of variables such as location or the person giving the command. Proofing is a necessity of the training process because dogs don't inherently generalize.

People are amazing at generalizing. Dogs aren't. For example, if the only place you ever train your puppy the *Leave It* command is in your kitchen with kibble, your puppy doesn't know to generalize that command to other environments, such as out on the street where a half-eaten burger is on the pavement. Your puppy will only know that *Leave It* means leave it when *you* say it in the *kitchen* with *kibble*.

You see there are *three variables* there: *who* is giving the command, *where* it's taking place, and the *specifics*.

Now your goal is to get your puppy to generalize. You want them to learn that *Leave It* means leave that thing alone, no matter *where* we are, and no matter *who's* telling you, and no matter what *it* is.

The way you get a puppy to generalize is by proofing. To proof a behavior, your puppy needs to be able to do it consistently in three to five different locations, and with all members of the household.

So, throughout this chapter, if you're teaching *Sit* in the living room, once your puppy is learning the behavior well, have all other members of your household also take a turn training *Sit*. And switch to other places in and around your home.

TRAINING TIPS

Gestures before words: Puppies learn hand gestures before they learn words. Always use verbal training commands with the gestures, understanding that at first they are only paying attention to the gesture. By association, over time they will learn the words.

Don't repeat: Say a command *once* and only once. If you say, "Down . . . down . . . come on, lie down . . . down," then *that* is the command they will learn. If they don't act after you say the word once, resist the urge to repeat it. Once your puppy starts to learn a new command, it is a good idea to wait a full 30 seconds before repeating it. Give their brain a chance to problem solve and figure it out on their own.

Remain upbeat: Speak all commands matter-of-factly or with a happy, fun tone of voice, and never with anger, shouting, or frustration. If you are feeling frustrated, don't let it show, don't let your puppy know.

Keep calm: Never get angry at your puppy for not learning as fast as you want them to learn.

Keep it brief: Five minutes is a perfectly solid amount of time for a training session for a puppy. Don't go longer. You can do 10 five-minute sessions per day. But keep each session brief.

Pay attention to their attention span: If your puppy loses focus or spaces out, you've likely trained for too long or you need to switch to a new treat.

Always train on an empty stomach: You're using treats as a reward, and they'll be vastly less motivating if your puppy just ate.

Avoid distractions when learning something new: You can add them in later, on purpose, when you want to make it more challenging.

Never use your hand to put your dog into position: It slows down the learning process. Stick to Lure and Bait.

End on a high note: Always end each training session on a high note. We teach the concept of the "jackpot," which is simply a handful of treats instead of a single treat. If your puppy's been having a hard time getting a certain behavior, but finally succeeds, don't just reward it, jackpot it. Jackpots are also perfect for ending a session; wait for them to nail the behavior and then reward with a jackpot and call it a wrap.

Essential Training Commands

Now that you understand the fundamentals of training, you're ready to learn the 6 key commands.

1. NAME GAME

 Purpose: To teach your puppy their name and to focus on you

This game reinforces the idea that you are awesome. You are always at the top and always worth paying attention to, regardless of what else is going on around your puppy.

For this training, you are going to need mild distractions. If your puppy isn't paying attention to you at all, your environment is too distracting; find somewhere else.

Step 1: Place your puppy on a leash, an arm's length away—not the full length of the leash. It doesn't matter if they are standing, sitting, or lying down. You should be able to touch the tip of their nose while you remain standing, or seated if you're unable to stand.

Step 2: **If you have a helper**, the other person should create a mild distraction such as walking through the room or making a noise from another room such as crinkling a bag or coughing or bouncing a ball (any noise other than calling the dog's name).

If you are solo, set up your training area where there are naturally occurring distractions such as a yard with distant squirrels or passing delivery trucks.

Step 3: As soon as your puppy turns their attention to the distraction, immediately call their name once—only once—in a happy voice.

Step 4: If they whip their head to look in the general vicinity of your face, say Yes (verbal marker) and give them a treat.

Training Tips

Troubleshooting: If they don't look at you when you say their name, put a treat in front of their nose so they can smell it, then pull it up to your eyes. You should be standing straight up or sitting, not down at their level. Once they look up at you, say Yes and give the treat.

Repetition: Do two to five minutes of repetitions of this game during each session, which you can repeat several times throughout the day. This game should be upbeat and fast paced.

Keep it simple: Only use *one* name for your puppy, not a bunch of different pet names. For a puppy, it's too confusing to learn different commands and names. When they're older, your dog will learn via context and repetition that "Snowflake" and "Snowy" and "Snowball" and "Snow Snow" are all meant for them, but for now, just pick one.

2. SIT

 Purpose: To teach your puppy to stop and be still

The classic demonstration of a trained dog is one who sits on command. But like all good manners, a *Sit* is more than a display of obedience; it truly comes in handy as a calming device to gain your puppy's focus and transition them from freeform play to paying attention.

Step 1: Select a training environment with no distractions. Place a treat in your hand and put it in front of your puppy's nose. Don't hold it too high or they'll be tempted to jump up. Keep your fist closed so they don't try to take it from your fingers. Don't worry, they can still smell it.

Step 2: Say the word *Sit* just once as you move your hand at a height just over their head, parallel to the ground, in a straight line forward to their butt. This motion forces them to either sit or back up.

If they sit (and this includes the "puppy sit" which is a goofy awkward sit with hips splayed out to the side) say *Yes* and give a treat, followed by joyful, effusive praise and affection.

If they back up, don't be frustrated, just give your nonresponse marker (*Ah ah*) and start over with Step 1.

If they jump up toward your hand, give your nonresponse marker (*Ah ah*) and withdraw the treat. Never reward your dog in any way when they are jumping up or don't have all four paws on the floor.

Step 3: Most dogs naturally exit the sit with the excitement of treat and praise, in which case you're all set to repeat Steps 1 and 2. But if they remain sitting, back up a few steps, pat your knees and call their name, and they will come over. Then go back to Steps 1 and 2.

Training Tips

Repetition: Repeat the training for about five minutes. You can do this a few times each day.

Stay positive: As with training any new behavior, your puppy is going to cycle through all kinds of responses to find out which one gets your approval. Your job is to let them know through your use of the verbal marker and the nonresponse marker. They're trying to learn. Don't get frustrated or angry. And don't reward until they figure it out, which might even be by accident.

Don't push them into position: Resist the urge to push their butt down. Don't ever push them into position as this will slow down the learning process and will likely cause them to begin shying away from your hands.

Jackpot it: If they're having a hard time, you can jackpot their very first successful sit to help cement the association that this is what you're talking about. The first time is always the hardest, and each subsequent sit will happen faster and with less confusion from your puppy.

Don't reward a half-sit: If their butt isn't on the ground, no dice.

But do be aware that some breeds, like Greyhounds, Boxers, and Pit Bulls, have rather petite rear ends so their butts only just barely touch the ground. That's okay. For such breeds, that counts as a sit.

Change the scenery: As with all commands, remember the importance of proofing. Practice *Sit* in other places.

3. DOWN

> Purpose: To teach your dog basic manners and patience

Once your dog knows *Sit*, you can proceed to *Down*.

Step 1: Put your dog into a sit. Remember, hold a treat in your hand and guide it back over your puppy's head to lead them into the sit.

Step 2: Put a treat right in front of your puppy's nose and say *Down* only one time as you very, very slowly pull it straight down perpendicular toward the ground, then toward you along the ground, making an L shape. (A diagonal motion doesn't work as well, as it will tend to make your puppy walk forward.) You have to go very slowly so they are so focused on the treat that they stop paying attention to what their body is doing. If you go too fast, they will stand up and go forward for the treat. Your puppy should be sniffing and licking your hand the whole time as you lure them down.

Step 3: When they slide into a down position, give the verbal marker *Yes* and then give them the treat and plenty of glorious praise.

Training Tips

Be patient: Most puppies won't get this right away. They'll stand up. That's okay. Don't get frustrated, or if you are frustrated, don't let it show. Just start over with Step 1.

Troubleshooting: If they remain in a sit, keep the treat on the ground for a few seconds to see if they will slide down. If they give up by putting their head in the air and ignoring the treat, you might have gone too fast. Try again, with the tasty treat right on their nose.

Don't push them into position: Resist any urge to push your dog down into position; they will resist against the push and the learning process will take much longer.

Popups are A-OK: Something we often hear is that a puppy did slide into down position, but then hopped right back up before the treat could be given. That's okay. Perfectly normal. Your puppy *did* do what you asked them to do: they did slide down. So, err on the side of rewarding the behavior. Give them the treat if they did a down, even if they popped back up. Don't worry. Later on, you can move to rewarding the duration, only giving the treat when they go down and stay down for a few seconds.

4. OFF

> ➔ Purpose: To stop your puppy from jumping on people or furniture

When teaching *Off*, many people accidentally say *Down* when they mean *Off*. Don't get them confused, or your puppy will get confused. You recently taught them what *Down* means. *Off* is something else entirely. Only use *Off* to mean "keep all four paws on the floor," or in other words, don't jump up.

When Your Puppy Jumps Up on You

Step 1: Say *Off* once, in a matter-of-fact and not angry tone.

Step 2: Immediately turn your back to your puppy, depriving them of your attention.

Step 3: When you sense or peek around and see that all four of their paws are on the floor, turn around and greet them again to see if this time they'll keep four paws on the floor instead of jumping. If they keep four-on-the-floor, give them praise and affection but keep it low key. Don't be overelaborate in your petting or enthusiasm, or your puppy might get so aroused they will start jumping again. No treats are needed: Your attention is all the reward they need. If they jump up on you again, go back to Step 1.

Training Tips

Negative attention is still attention: If they keep jumping up, walk away and do something else. Don't give them eye contact or any attention of any kind. *To a puppy, negative attention is still attention.* The best way for them to learn not to jump is through ignoring them until they have four-on-the-floor.

Including other people: If a friend is coming over, make arrangements in advance. Let your friend know to behave exactly as in Steps 1 to 3 when they arrive. If your puppy jumps on your friend, say Off once, and at this point your friend should turn their back and ignore the puppy. If your friend shouts no or pushes the puppy down or anything like that, that goes in the category of negative attention still being attention. Your puppy will have associated jumping with a kind of rewarding play activity, the "I jump and you push and shout" game. Optionally, you could leash your puppy before guests come over to have an added level of control, but do not use the leash to jerk or yank your puppy.

When Your Puppy Jumps on Furniture

Let's assume you don't want your puppy on your sofa. This applies equally to a bed or counter or any other furniture. A bit of advance planning helps: if you're not wearing a treat bag on your hip at all times, then stash a plastic baggie full of treats in an end table near the sofa.

Step 1: If you're sitting on the sofa and your puppy jumps up, give the nonresponse marker *Ah ah* and reach for a treat.

Step 2: Stand up and say *Off* once as you toss a treat to the floor, away from the sofa.

Step 3: When your puppy jumps down, say *Yes* and they'll proceed to help themselves to the treat. Follow up with plenty of praise and affection. You are teaching them that whatever joy there was in jumping up on the sofa or bed to be with you, there's way more joy to be had by listening to you when you say *Off*.

5. WAIT

> → Purpose: Countless uses throughout the day when you need your dog to hold still and wait calmly for their safety or your convenience or peace of mind

Before proceeding, we should explain how *Wait* is different from *Stay*. *Wait* is incredibly versatile, for the myriad times you'd like them to be polite and patient, such as waiting calmly to get their dinner, or pausing at the door instead of bolting out, or not jumping out of the car and potentially into ongoing traffic. In a *Wait*, your puppy remains calmly in position until you release them with a release word.

Stay is used in formal obedience and rarely used in day-to-day life. A dog in a *Stay* must remain in that position until you come back to them. It means "I'm leaving, don't move, I'll be back." For this reason, in this book we're teaching *Wait* but not *Stay*.

Verbal release word: In order to teach *Wait*, you will need a new kind of marker, a verbal release word. Many people use "Okay," but we advise against it because puppies hear you use this word all the time, so it lacks specialness. We like the words "free" and "release." We'll use the word *Free* as the verbal release word in this book. Whatever you choose, remember to always be consistent.

Wait Until Dinner

To teach *Wait*, the optimal time is dinnertime. Your puppy should be good and hungry.

Step 1: Take your dog's food bowl off the floor and fill it with their dinner. Walk over to where they usually eat.

Step 2: While holding the bowl in one hand, with your other hand put your puppy into a *Sit* or a *Down* (*Sit* is most common). As a reminder, you'll hold a treat in your hand and guide it back over your puppy's head to lead them into the sit. They should be arm's length from the bowl.

Step 3: Give the hand gesture of a flat palm toward the puppy's face like a stop signal and say *Wait* once and only once.

Step 4: With your puppy now sitting politely, put the bowl down.

Step 5: If they break the sit, use your nonresponse marker (*Ah ah*) and pull the food bowl back up off the floor. Reset by putting them back into a sit (Step 2). Repeat Steps 2 to 5 as many times as needed, keeping very matter-of-fact and without showing any hint of frustration. Whatever you do, don't allow them to eat their food until you have put the bowl down and stood up straight with them remaining in the sit position.

Step 6: If they stay sitting while you stand back up, give the release word *Free*, and they should now go enjoy their dinner. You don't need to say Yes or give a treat; dinner is their reward.

Training Tips

Troubleshooting: If your puppy doesn't release when you say Free, tap on the food bowl and say, "It's okay, you can eat!" Keep it happy, cheerful, and encouraging. In a moment they'll come over and dine.

Be prepared: Most commonly, the moment you put that bowl on the floor your puppy is going to break their sit and try to bury their face in the bowl. Do your utmost to not let that happen; be nimble and at the ready to snatch that bowl back up off the floor. But if they do rush past your defenses and manage to snag a few pieces of kibble, that's okay. Don't despair, but pull the bowl up anyway, as that Wait just wasn't good enough. It's back to Step 2.

Additional Training Opportunities

Proofing: Now that you've taught Wait at mealtime, you can move on to proofing the command in other situations using the same principles and process.

Getting into the car: For example, if your puppy loves going for rides in the car, use *Wait* to make sure they sit and wait politely for you to first open the car door and then say *Free*. If they break their *Sit*, say *Ah ah*, close the door, and start again. If they manage to actually jump into the car, say *Ah ah*, take them out of the car by picking them up or calling them. Once they're out of the car, close the car door again, put them back into a *Sit*, then *Wait*, then slowly open the door again as you start anew. Your puppy must learn that if they are going to get what they want—a car ride—they are going to have to go about it the right way: your way.

Getting out of the car: Use the same procedure when you arrive at your destination. Don't let your puppy bolt out of the car. Instead, open the door just a crack and say *Wait*. Slowly begin to open the door. If they break their sit or down, say *Ah ah*, then gently close the door and start over. They don't get to exit the car until you've put the leash on and exclaimed *Free*. If they manage to jump out before you give the command, have them jump back into the car or place them there, and then say *Wait*. As with getting into the car, they need to get it right in order to get what they want.

Find other opportunities: You can proof *Wait* in countless scenarios—any time when the action that follows the *Wait* will be super enjoyable and rewarding.

6. LEAVE IT

> → Purpose: To prevent your dog from ingesting something they shouldn't, like dropped food, toys, bones, garbage, or medication

Life is full of temptations, little and large, and most of them end up on the ground right under your puppy's nose. Your puppy is a naturally curious scavenger only too happy to gobble up everything from bones to pills to poop, so the *Leave It* command is the key to their safety and your sanity.

Leave It is an anticipatory command, to prevent your puppy from putting something in their mouth. It's different than *Drop It*, which we covered in Preventing Food Aggression.

Proofing required: Because it's so important for safety, *Leave It* should be proofed in as many types of scenarios as possible: in your kitchen where there might be dropped bones or raw chicken; in your bathroom where dangerous pills could fall to the floor; in a living room where ingesting a LEGO could be a danger; or out on walks where rotten old food or garbage might be smeared on the sidewalk.

Distractions are okay: In training *Leave It*, it doesn't matter if the environment is distracting, as the treats you'll be using will command your puppy's attention. For that reason, we remind you to use incredibly tasty small, soft, meat treats, and never biscuits or cookies that crumble nor kibble that is much less rewarding.

Phase 1: Covered Treat

We begin with a simple game in which your puppy must forgo a treat hidden under your shoe in favor of a more compelling treat you'll provide from your hand.

> **Step 1:** Stand up. It's best if your puppy is standing or sitting. Wear shoes—no sandals, flip-flops, or bare feet.

> **Step 2:** Take a treat from your pouch. Show your puppy that you have a delicious treat in your hand, and let them watch you as put that treat under your shoe and step on it, fully covering it. Your puppy must see you do this and understand that you left a treat under your shoe and that it is no longer in your hand. If they know it's there, they will start pawing at your shoe and sniffing around, trying to figure out how to get at the covered treat. If they don't try to get at the treat, they might have missed the hide, so move your foot off to the side and tap the ground near the treat to direct

their attention to it. Then quickly cover it with your shoe before they can snag it.

Step 3: Say *Leave It* once and only once in a happy tone of voice. They will keep trying to get at the treat, getting more and more frustrated. At some point—and this could take 20 seconds or a few minutes—they will look up at you purely out of frustration and confusion.

Step 4: Then, and only then, exclaim *Yes* and give them a treat from your hand. Do not under any circumstances give them the one from under your shoe.

> **Be patient:** Don't repeat the command. It literally could take several minutes for them to look up at you. Remain vigilant so you notice immediately once they do so. They most likely will. Be patient. If they don't, see the Troubleshooting tip here.

Step 5: Take your foot off the treat. Tap the ground with your foot so they can see the treat is visible again, then quickly, before they can get to the treat, cover it back up with your foot. Now repeat Steps 3 and 4.

Step 6: Repeat Step 5 a few more times. You should notice that your puppy is getting quicker, figuring it out. They should now very rapidly be giving up on the foot treat and looking up at you or ignoring the treat altogether.

Troubleshooting: Some puppies are less food driven or more easily distractible, and either could result in your puppy not having the drive to look up at you for the treat. These puppies will typically start by pawing at your shoe and then they will stop trying to get that treat from under your shoe. For this puppy, say *Yes* when they stop going for the treat. They have indeed left it, and you should now reward them with a treat. If this is your puppy, throughout *Leave It* training, reward them when they stop going for the off-limits treat instead of when they look up at you.

Phase 2: Exposed Treat

We now make the game a bit more realistic by displaying the forbidden treat right out in the open, no longer hidden under your shoe.

> **Step 1:** Now that they know the game, tap the ground with your foot, but this time don't cover the treat with your foot. Just keep your foot very near or hovering. Wait for your puppy to look at the exposed treat.
>
> **Step 2:** As soon as they look at the treat but before they make any move toward it, say *Leave It*. If they look up at you, reward them with *Yes* and a treat from your hand. If they go for the one on the floor, cover it quickly with your foot and don't reward them until they look back at you.
>
>> **Establish success before moving on:** You're changing the rules to make it ever more difficult. It might take them a few tries to realize the rules have changed. Don't move on until Phase 2 is a lock. If your puppy sometimes goes for the floor treat, stay with Phase 2.

Phase 3: Increasing the Difficulty

Now it gets really fun as you up the ante. The game remains the same, but the stakes are higher.

> **Step 1:** Give them a pile of treats on the floor that they have to resist and look up at you instead. It's harder to say no to 10 treats

than to one treat. When using a pile of treats, you can use your feet or hands to cover them up and prevent your puppy from getting them. You can also ask a friend to help. In this example, the reward should be a jackpot of the same kind of treats (dogs can't count, so it doesn't have to be the exact number), or a couple of significantly more delectable treats.

Step 2: Mix it up by using different treats, or a combination of treats. But still the same game.

Step 3: Put the treat or handful of treats even closer to the puppy, right by their paws. Same game; you're just pushing their willpower to the limits. Try having them do *Leave It* from a down position with treats being moved closer and closer to their paws and nose.

Step 4: Repeat these same phases in the kitchen, bathroom, family room, and other rooms. Train it in your car. Out on walks it's especially important. Remember to bring treats with you at all times so you can practice *Leave It* right out on the sidewalk.

Training Tips

Always trade up: The treat in your hand must always be equal to or better than the treat on the ground. Your puppy is learning that by leaving alone this one object of their desire, they get something that is just as good or even better.

Dropping food: Since it's not uncommon for us to occasionally drop a piece of food, this real-world example provides a helpful illustration of the key principles of *Leave It*. Imagine this scenario: you accidentally drop a piece of juicy roast turkey on the kitchen floor. Your puppy is incredibly aroused by the aroma, and you think quickly and say *Leave It*. If your puppy obeys the command, this is truly an astonishing feat of willpower, and one you should immediately reward. Say *Yes* right away, but what treat are you going to give them? Is there a treat in your arsenal that is a trade up from the succulent turkey? Not really. So, pick up the piece of turkey from the floor, tear off a couple small pieces, and give them to your puppy. Their performance of *Leave It* in this situation was worthy of such a regal treat. (As for the dropped turkey, we suggest cutting it up into pieces and storing it in the refrigerator to use as training treats later on.)

STEP 7

leash walking and coming when called

While Step 7 is a continuation of Step 6—the basic training commands and behaviors your puppy should learn early on—we're breaking these biggies into their own step for good reason.

At the Zoom Room, we cover loose leash walking and coming when called during our puppy training and our obedience training classes, but over the years we saw two reasons to create special workshops just for these behaviors: safety and difficulty.

First, there's *safety*. These behaviors are crucial to maintaining the basic control necessary for the safety of your dog, other people, and yourself.

But the biggest reason is how much *difficulty* most people have with them. We couldn't count the number of times we've had dog owners visit us saying, "My dog is really well behaved, except . . ." And this sentence always ends with either ". . . they pull on their leash" or ". . . they don't always come when I call their name." Clearly these behaviors come up many times every day for puppy and dog owners, and they present a real challenge. And we're therefore going to show them a little extra love.

Puppy Perspective

When a puppy ventures out on a walk, they want to explore the world primarily through the sense of smell, and to do so in an outward-moving circular pattern. They are eager to explore, and this eagerness can and will take the form of dragging you along, unless you teach them that walks are vastly more enjoyable when they stick to your side.

All dogs have what's called an oppositional reflex. What this means is that their bodies will reflexively move away from any applied pressure. You have this reflex, too. If someone grabs you by the lapels and pulls you, you will instinctively pull away. Dogs, including puppies, most commonly exhibit this reflex when walking on a leash.

When your dog feels pressure on their collar, they will reflexively surge forward, into the pressure. The harder you pull back, the harder your dog will pull forward. Mushers use the oppositional reflex to their advantage. Pulling back on the leads is what causes the sled dogs to pull, pull, pull.

Unless you are mushing sled dogs, oppositional reflex isn't your friend. In this step, you'll learn how to avoid it. Using a front-clip harness is one of the most effective methods. The oppositional reflex kicks in when you use a flat-buckle collar or a back-clip harness. However, when your puppy pulls forward in a *front-clip harness*, the design causes them to be turned sideways, toward you. This prevents the oppositional reflex from being triggered and helps stop the pulling.

Dogs also have an innate desire to circle their territory, smelling everything along the way as they move in an outward trajectory. This will come in handy during loose leash training.

As to coming when called, since you two have mastered the Name Game, and since they are well acquainted with your awesomeness, they should be well motivated to dash to your every beck and call. But there are so very many interesting things going on in their life, so practicing the training recommended here will help cement the recall command.

Loose Leash Walking

→ Purpose: For the safety of your dog, other people, and yourself; and to enjoy better control

While there are more advanced levels of loose leash walking, our goal here is to set up the key foundational learning for your puppy that walking with you and by your side is enjoyable and inherently rewarding.

You should first teach loose leash walking in a more abstract training setting at home, off leash. Once this is mastered you can move on to the second phase: using a leash at home. Finally, you'll progress to the third phase: working on this skill while out on an actual walk.

PHASE 1: PRACTICE AT HOME

We'll begin by encouraging your puppy to follow you around, sticking close to you, as it's within this happy bubble that all good things happen. This lays the foundation for their remaining by your side during walks.

> **Step 1:** Select a large room or a yard, anywhere that you can move freely about, walking both forward and backward, without any worry about bumping into things. Your puppy is off leash.
>
> **Step 2:** Walk around, clapping and patting your knees and hollering, "Come on! Yay!" or something similar. There's no specific command, you simply want your puppy to follow you around as you remain in constant motion.
>
> **Step 3:** As your puppy comes to you and stays in a happy, three-foot-radius bubble around you, give them a treat and continue to praise them and talk happily to them and give treats to them as you continue on your forward and backward journey through the space. Be mindful of your own safety.

Training Tips

Keep moving while you hand out treats: You are rewarding them for staying near you while you're in motion. Be generous with your treats, doling them out as you continue your follow-the-leader game around the room. You want your puppy to think of that three-foot bubble around you as a fantastically rewarding place to be.

Kibble is a fine choice: If it's right before mealtime, consider hand-feeding your puppy their entire meal of kibble while walking around in this way. Normally, when you're teaching them a new behavior, you want to train with high-value treats, not ordinary kibble. But in this case, you're not training a new behavior, you're rewarding something that is inherently fun; your puppy will naturally enjoy following you around, especially if you approach this with playfulness and joy and lots of happy verbal praise as you move around the room. In addition, high-value training treats are higher in calories, and since you'll be giving out so many of them during these follow-the-leader sessions, using kibble will keep the calorie count down. Lastly, by hand-feeding, you are also promoting bonding.

Up your treat game: If they aren't coming or staying in your happy bubble, take it up a notch by skipping the kibble, using a much more desirable treat, and rewarding more frequently.

PHASE 2: ADD A LEASH

Once your puppy is doing wonderfully with this game, add a leash into the mix. If you're using the house line, just pick up the loose end and use it like a leash. You should save this phase until after they've mastered Phase 1.

Equipment: Use a six-foot leash or an eight-foot house line. Avoid retractable leashes, which can cause injury, provide a false sense of control, and drag on the ground and frighten a puppy. (See Puppy Supplies Checklist, for a refresher on leash choice.)

No yanking: The steps are the exact same as in Phase 1. Just be sure not to yank the leash. A gentle tug is okay, but if you yank the leash, your puppy's oppositional reflex will kick in, and they will lean back away and against the pull, or may come to dislike the leash.

Practice with the house line: In addition to Phases 1 and 2, we also recommend you let your puppy wear the house line around your home even when you're not actively training loose leash walking. This lets them get used to being on a leash.

House line safety: For your puppy's safety, be sure to remove the house line when you leave home or can't actively pay attention to your puppy. Don't improvise a house line with any old rope or cord, as it could alter your dog's gait and impede them from safely dragging it around your home. Stick to one specifically designed for this purpose.

PHASE 3: ON WALKS

Now your puppy is ready to venture outside on an actual walk. Your puppy is excited to explore, and you use that to your advantage by heading backward if they're not sticking by your side.

Equipment: Front-clip harness, six-foot leash.

Harness required: During your first walks, always keep your puppy in a front-clip harness. It helps teach them loose leash walking, as when they try to pull, it will turn them sideways and toward you instead of a rearing-up position.

Step 1: With your puppy leashed, head out on your walk. They should stay near your side with a loose leash. As long as they're keeping a loose leash, create a perfect love bubble around you, communicating to your puppy that being near you is where all good things happen. This means praising them, saying "good dog," and giving out treats from your treat pouch, enlivening the walk with lots of praise and attention. Reward very frequently as long as they stay near your side—within a few feet.

Step 2: If they pull, immediately turn around and walk three steps back in the direction you came from.

Stop and wait if they won't go back: If your puppy won't go back three steps with you, which is understandable as they really don't want to cover ground they've already covered, don't drag them back. Instead just stop and wait there for a while. It's actually a good sign that they don't want to go back; it means your training is working. As soon as they stop pulling, head forward again, as in Step 1.

Step 3: Turn around again, facing the direction you intend to go, and make sure they're calm and under control. If not, ask them for a *Sit*, guiding a treat back over their head to lead them into the *Sit* if they don't automatically do it on command. Remember to always reward the *Sit* with treats.

Step 4: Once they're under control with no pressure on the leash, resume your walk in the original direction. There's no need for a verbal marker or a treat, as getting to go forward again is the reward. You're now back at Step 1.

Training Tips

Dogs favor circular patterns for maximum novelty: There's something important about your puppy you should know in order to understand why we're training loose leash walking using backward steps. Dogs are migratory creatures who instinctively desire to move forward in a circle around their territory. They want to smell everything in an outward-moving path. When you take them three steps backward, it is pretty frustrating. You're asking them to retrace the same path they've already sniffed when they would rather be venturing farther out. You are teaching them that the only way to go forward is to do so calmly by your side, without pulling.

Off-Leash Dog Parks

We can't stress this enough: for puppies, an off-leash dog park must be fully enclosed with no risk of your puppy bolting.

As long as it is enclosed, your puppy is able to visit an off-leash dog park as soon as they are fully vaccinated.

But should you go? It depends. Dog parks are generally intended for adult dogs, and the only thing you can reasonably expect is to expect the unexpected; you can't predict what kind of dogs will show up on any given day. For example, some dogs love to chase, which your puppy might not enjoy. Nor can you expect what kind of dog *owners* will be present. Will they be attentive and responsible? If you're overly concerned, finding a great puppy play space near you (see **Puppy Play Spaces**) will always be a safer bet.

If you do bring your fully vaccinated puppy to an off-leash dog park, here's what you need to know:

- You must be vigilant at all times; keep your eyes off your phone and on your puppy.
- If your puppy appears shy, nervous, or stressed, it's time to leave.
- If there's a big mismatch between your puppy and the size and energy level of the other dogs, it's time to go.
- In short, if your puppy isn't having the time of their life, call it a day.

Something else we have learned about dog parks is that many people inadvertently ruin their dog's recall training. We have some great tips to ensure this doesn't happen to you.

The rule is simple: at the dog park, never call your puppy to come to you. When you want them, go get your puppy. You walk to them; you don't call them to you.

If you're wondering why, it's because your puppy is probably in the middle of an amazingly fun interaction with other dogs, running, playing, and having a great time. By calling you are breaking two of the cardinal rules of Come When Called.

First, remember you don't want to use *Come* when there is an excessive amount of distraction. Dog owners who attempt this at the dog park end up sounding like this: "Come here, come, come, come here, Max, Maxie, come Maxie come, come here, Max." And remember you only want to say the command once.

Second, you never want *Come* to be punitive. Since they're having a fabulous day, if you do a recall command and then take them away from the park, they will feel that they are being punished. The next time you ask them to come, they will think twice.

Coming When Called

> Purpose: For your dog's safety and your convenience

You are now going to teach your puppy a recall for no reason. They'll learn to come when you call them. Even though you have no specific need to do so, they'll learn this command for when you *do* have good reason.

Of all training commands, this one can feel the most punitive to a puppy, as generally puppies are always doing exactly what they want to be doing, be it playing, lying in the sun, or whatever floats their boat, and you're asking them to put an end to that enjoyable activity.

Wait for the right moment: For starters, don't practice *Come* when your puppy is doing something super awesome, such as playing with another dog. Set yourself up for success by relying on minor distractions, life's little pleasures.

Don't bum them out: Never use a recall for something punitive or unpleasant. Your puppy was in a happy place, and you call them over to scold them or take them to the vet or trim their nails. They'll wonder why they ever listened to *Come*, and this can interfere with the training.

Step 1: Your puppy should be mildly otherwise engaged. Say your puppy's name to get their attention. They already mastered the Name Game, so they should look up at you. You don't need to be far away; a recall from 10 feet away is still a recall.

Step 2: Exclaim *Come* in an excited voice. You can add clapping or thigh slapping. Horses and dogs are the two animals who respond positively to percussive sounds like these. They should scamper over to you.

Step 3: As soon as they come over, say *Yes*.

Step 4: Grasp your puppy's collar and give them a treat. By

holding their collar, you teach them that *Come* means to come hang out with you. You don't want them to just "dine and dash," snatching their treat and then skedaddling back to their previous activity. Now that they've come over, they should get lots of attention, treats, praise, petting, and joy.

Training Tips

If you are solo: At the end of the training session you can't reset and repeat, as now that your puppy is happily by your side, they will follow you around. If you want to keep working on recall, turn your attention to something else; go check your e-mail or fold clothes. Once your puppy has trotted off to lie down or do something else, *then* you can go back to Step 1 and repeat.

If you have a helper: If there is at least one other person present, you can extend the training by having each person take a handful of treats and spread out to different locations in your home. The first person should follow Steps 1 to 4. Once this is done, the next person should do Steps 1 to 4. And so on, in round robin, for up to a maximum of five minutes.

Make sure they know their name: If your dog doesn't look up when you say their name, go back to training the *Name Game*.

Sell it with enthusiasm: If they don't come when you call them, try a higher voice or more excitement, more clapping, more rustling the treat bag—you can whoop and holler all you'd like. With delicious enough treats, enough verbal excitement, and ensuring they weren't doing anything too earth-shattering to begin with, they will come. If they are still more interested in their activity than in coming to you, don't try to force the *Come*. Instead, halt the exercise and wait until a time your puppy is doing something less interesting, and then try again.

Exercising Your Puppy

While we're talking about walking around with your puppy and their bounding toward the sound of your voice, this seems a fitting time to raise the important issue of physical exercise. The average dog in America does not get enough exercise. So many behavioral issues can be eliminated simply by increasing the amount of physical activity. As we often say, "A tired dog is a happy dog," by which we really mean that a tired dog is a well-behaved one.

What Counts as Exercise?

Before your puppy has had all of their vaccinations, you will need to limit their exposure, so your options are fewer.

- Walking around the backyard (on or off leash)
- Walking around the house
- Playing fetch or tug
- Attending a safe puppy play space (see **Puppy Play Spaces**)

Once your puppy has all of their shots, your best bet will always be going for a walk. Walks provide an excellent activity level, promote bonding between you and your pup, play to your puppy's migratory nature, and provide ongoing opportunities for improving obedience training such as loose leash walking.

What Not to Do

- You should not view a visit to doggy day care as a form of exercise for your puppy. Think of day care as "recess" (unstructured play) and a walk as "P.E." (continuous and disciplined physical activity with a specified goal).
- Your puppy should never jog with you until they are fully grown and your vet has explicitly given you clearance to go jogging together.

How Much Exercise?

- Three shorter walks are always better than one long one.

- Puppies need more and more exercise as they get older.
- Larger breeds need more exercise than smaller breeds.
- Working and sporting dogs need more exercise than toy breeds and lap dogs.
- Puppies from working lineages need more exercise than those from confirmation lineages (in case this is unclear, that means a German Shepherd whose parents are working or hunting dogs needs more exercise than a German Shepherd whose parents are show dogs).
- Medium- and large-breed puppies can generally walk a total of about one mile per day for each month of their age, so a four-month-old medium-breed puppy could walk a total of four miles each day, divided into a minimum of two separate walks.

preparing for the future

By the time you've mastered all seven steps, you might be wondering, what's next? It's an excellent question, and the answer is that by no means do you need to stop there. Your puppy has mastered the basics and is now approaching adolescence. There are some truly wonderful activities you and your puppy can take part in together.

American Kennel Club's S.T.A.R. Puppy® Program

The American Kennel Club offers a wonderful designation, S.T.A.R. (Socialization, Training, Activity, Responsibility), for puppies. There's a checklist of 20 items that you and your puppy must accomplish to receive this designation. It includes the key ingredients for responsible pet ownership, as well as the fundamental socialization and training efforts needed to ensure a happy, healthy, well-adjusted pup. See Resources for a link to learn more.

Advanced Training

In The Six Key Commands and Leash Walking and Coming When Called, we focused on seven of the most important commands that your puppy should learn: Name Game, *Sit*, *Down*, *Off*, *Wait*, *Leave It*, and *Come*. Once you've mastered these, there are many additional more advanced behaviors you can train using the exact same principle of consistently rewarding the desired behavior.

You can also learn how to sequence. Sequencing is when you train a dog to first do A, then B, then C, etc. If you ever see a dog in a movie do some amazing feat, that's exactly how the behavior was trained: through sequencing.

Here's a small handful of additional behaviors you can teach your puppy once they're a bit older and have mastered the basics:

- **Go to Your Bed** (also known as a boundary stay)
- **Speak/Shush** (bark on command, stop barking on command)
- **Touch** (the crucial command needed to teach most dog tricks)
- **Tricks** (there are too many to list, but they build upon **Touch** and the concept of sequencing)
- **Paw** (a classic, to shake hands)
- **Retrieve/Fetch**
- **Stay** (including more advanced versions with longer duration, distance, and distractions; these can also be done with **Wait**)
- **Watch Me** (to help your dog focus on you and ignore distractions)

Dog Sports

There are some exciting dog sports you and your puppy might enjoy. We've provided a short list of some of the dog sports we especially love to teach at the Zoom Room. We approach these as less about competition and more about finding opportunities to deepen the bonds of communication between you and your puppy.

You might also encounter some others such as Barn Hunt, Earth Dog, and Lure Coursing, but our list is focused on sporting activities that you can engage in *with* your dog, celebrating companionship.

- **Dog Agility:** you and your dog navigate an obstacle course

- **Flyball:** fast-paced action in which your dog dashes back and forth chasing a launched ball

- **Rally Obedience:** takes the skills of obedience and turns them into a game with specified stations and an emphasis on precision

- **Urban Herding:** also called Treibball, this activity is like herding sheep, but indoors, where dogs herd large exercise balls into soccer goals

- **Nosework/Scent:** fundamental search-and-rescue skills turned into games that hone your dog's ability to discriminate scents

When to Seek a Behaviorist or Trainer

In this book, we've tried to address the most common concerns and needs for the majority of new puppy owners. But throughout, we've touched on some behavioral issues that are beyond the scope of this book. While the fundamentals of positive reinforcement training in this book should afford you the ability to teach your puppy just about anything, certain problem behaviors are a cause for concern, and if they are present, we recommend you seek out a qualified behaviorist or dog trainer in your area who embraces positive training. These problem behaviors warrant getting help:

- Window barking (barking at every person or dog who walks past)

- Not getting along with other pets or family members

- Reactivity to other dogs

- Separation anxiety

- Fear of crate
- Fear of children
- Resource guarding (food, beds, toys, people)
- Destructive chewing
- Obsessive behaviors (spinning in circles, licking furniture)
- Biting humans or other dogs

Additionally, if your puppy has a disability such as deafness or blindness, how you socialize and train will change. We advise seeking professional help for dogs with disabilities.

And, lastly, if you follow the steps provided for any of the goals such as potty training, crate training, or basic commands, and they just aren't working, we'd also recommend that you seek outside help.

resources

Additional Reading

The Other End of the Leash by Patricia B. McConnell
The Truth About Dogs by Stephen Budiansky

Puppy-Friendly Places

Find a Zoom Room location near you: ZoomRoom.com/locations

Dog-centered meet-up groups: Meetup.com/find/?keywords=dog

Dog-friendly places from Yelp: Yelp.com/search?find_desc=%22dog+friendly&attrs=DogsAllowed

Dog-friendly places from BringFido.com: BringFido.com/attraction

Puppy Socialization

American Kennel Club S.T.A.R. Puppy® Program: AKC.org/products-services/training-programs/canine-good-citizen/akc-star-puppy

American Veterinary Medical Association's position on puppy socialization: AVMA.org/KB/Resources/LiteratureReviews/Pages/Welfare-Implications-of-Socialization-of-Puppies-and-Kittens.aspx

American Veterinary Society of Animal Behavior's Position Statement On Puppy Socialization: AVSAB.org/wp-content/uploads/2018/03/Puppy_Socialization_Position_Stateme

Dog Body Language

Zoom Room Guide to Dog Body Language: ZoomRoom.com/admin/guide-to-dog-body-language

Zoom Room Guide to Dog Play Gestures: ZoomRoom.com/admin/guide-to-dog-play-gestures

Puppy Health

Tips on health, nutrition, unbiased product reviews, and more: *Whole Dog Journal,* Whole-Dog-Journal.com

List of plants toxic to dogs: ASPCA.org/pet-care/animal-poison-control/dogs-plant-list

List of human foods poisonous to dogs: ASPCA.org/pet-care/animal-poison-control/people-foods-avoid-feeding-your-pets

Finding a Responsible Puppy Breeder

The Humane Society's guide: HumaneSociety.org/assets/pdfs/pets/puppy_mills/find_responsi

The American Kennel Club's guide: AKC.org/press-center/articles/responsible-breeders

ASPCA's position on puppy mills: ASPCA.org/animal-cruelty/puppy-mills/closer-look-puppy-mills-old

Resources for Finding and Adopting a Puppy

The Humane Society's guide on finding a puppy: HumaneSociety.org/resources/where-get-puppy

American Kennel Club's Guide to dog breeds: AKC.org/dog-breeds

AdoptAPet.com/adopt-a-shelter-puppy

ASPCA.org/adopt-pet/adoptable-dogs-your-local-shelter

PetFinder.com/animal-shelters-and-rescues